On
Re-Making
the World

Other books by Harry Schultz:

- A Treasury of Wall Street Wisdom
- How to Keep Your Money and Freedom
- The International Monetary Muddle
- Bear Markets—How to Survive and Make Money in Them (8 printings)
- Financial Tactics and Terms for the Sophisticated International Investor
- Panics and Crashes (4 revised editions)
- How the Experts Buy & Sell Gold Bullion, Gold Stocks & Gold Coins
- How You Can Profit from Gold
- Rules For Being a Flexible Investor and/or Trader
- Inflation and Inflation Hedges
- You and Gold
- Diccionario de finanzas y tacticas financieras
- The Dollar Devaluation—Mechanics and Timing
- Handbook for Using and Understanding Swiss Banks
- Harry Schultz's Bear Market Investment Strategies
- What Prudent Investors Should Know about Switzerland & Foreign Money Havens
- 1000 Days of Freedom?
- After A Crash—Bear Market Money Making

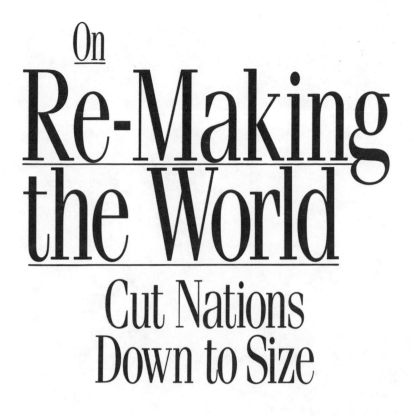

On
Re-Making
the World

Cut Nations
Down to Size

Harry D. Schultz

ICDWN

Silver Spring, Maryland

Printed in the United States of America

Published by:

International Commission for the
   De-Centralization of the World's Nations
P.O. Box 2376
Silver Spring, Maryland 20915, USA

ISBN 0-9630716-0-2

To the hope that closed minds can be opened.

Contents

Acknowledgments

Research & Contributing Editors: Gordon Frisch and Anton Keller.

Thanks also to Joyce Leicester for ideas and editing.

On-going research conducted by International Commission for the De-centralization of the World's Nations, Gordon Frisch, chairman.

Author's note: It took me four months and a whole lifetime to write this book. I've been writing it in my head for decades. Finally it burst forth explosively as a concept whose time had truly come and demanded the attention of the world.

In my opinion.

In My Opinion...

Edward Cummings wrote "A world is *made*—not born. ... listen! There's a hell of a good universe next door, let's go!" Ah... but there's the rub! There is no escape from birth or death in this world, so we must try to endure the interval between and make the best of it, not just for ourselves, but for *those who follow.*

On Re-making The World is one of the most remarkable books I have ever read! I could not believe the wisdom it expels. My old friend, Harry Schultz, has perhaps changed our future. This book blazes a trail where no one had the courage or imagination to go. Or maybe it's simply an idea whose time has come. In either case, it leads the way. It'll shock people, but it's needed.

When World War Two ended, there were about 50 countries in the world. Today, there are about 180. Until I read *On Re-making The World*, I erroneously thought the proliferation of new, smaller countries were an abomination. This book turned my thinking in a new, more perceptive direction. It made me remember that bigness does not mean greatness, in nations, any more than in people.

I recalled that every large-scale, centralized institution is clumsy and the only organization—whether it be companies, school systems, or nations—that function efficiently are those that are decentralized and segmented into small, easily-managed units. In the chessboard of the world, the pieces are the phenomena of the universe—the rules of the game. Harry has shown us the wisdom of redesigning the obese, stagnant, decaying land masses and revitalizing them.

On Re-making The World is not another backward glance over travelled roads. It is not the common reassembly of old, time-worn myths and theories, bundled with some new statistics, that are often passed off as a new book. Harry's book ploughs *new ground*. It passes, even surpasses, my standards for a *worthwhile* book.

Above all, it made me think. It is wholly-original, written in the author's unique style, wherein each page sparkles with new visions. It is as fatal as it is cowardly to blind ourselves to facts, because they are not to our taste. You'll never do this again after reading this new page-turner.

They say the definition of a good book is one that someone did not want written. No doubt many who do not want their sacred oxes gored will not like people to think about revolutionary change. I have long-known Harry Schultz to be a brave man, and only such a person could suggest such startling changes.

Leon D. Richardson
Chairman, Magna Industrial Co. Ltd.
Hong Kong International Headquarters

About this book...

Hallelujah! Harry Schultz has done it! As far as I know there are no books on the topic. It's one of the most intriguing subjects & covers momentous decision-making areas facing humanity.

- The subject: Self-determination. Let all peoples decide what govt. they live under. Why should a foreign entity decree that? Or a war?
- Some people, many of whom have never really thought it through, will respond: "Impractical! The world should go in the opposite direction, to one-worldism." If we were all one world, who would we fight? Answer: each other. More than ever. History proves that. Others will claim: "But nations need to be big, strong, powerful, rich & prosperous." Yeah! Like Switzerland, Hong Kong, Taiwan? Switzerland hasn't had a war in 200-300 years. Hong Kong is fabulously rich; the USSR is destitute. The Chinese are slaves. The Taiwanese are free.

There are some 30 wars going on in the world today. Almost all are rooted in religion, ethnicity, race. Why not allow such groups, such as in Canada & No. Ireland, although they are not yet actually at war, to secede and have their own countries?

Ethics and ethnicity, race and religion, cultures & economics, freedom & morality far outrank landmass & numbers. NOTHING out-ranks the freedom of self-determination. Meanwhile Emir Bush is dedicated to merging us all into a ONE WORLD conglomerate.

Harry O.T. (original thinker) Schultz publishes what I once called the world's No. 1 newsletter. And now he's come in first again, with an exciting new book, *On Re-Making the World*. Breaking new ground, he attacks rigid ideas on borders & bigness & wants to give separate country status to a lot of people who either need it desperately, or could benefit from it greatly. Lower taxes, a voice, & more freedom are the aims. Let people cut their nations down to size—the Baltics, Kurds, Yugoslavs. Re-design them all according to the wishes of their people, starting with the USSR & including the USA.

In govt., business, education, the answer is to privatize. Small is better than big. The bigger & more powerful a govt. is the FARTHER REMOVED FROM THE PEOPLE IT IS, the more dictatorial & crooked it is. Big Brother should do nothing for us that can be done as well or better by our families, by private interests, or by Little Brother & that includes practically everything. Big business gets ever richer & bigger not because of its efficiency primarily, but because of its incestuous, fascistic relationship with Big Brother, giving them a down-hill playing field. As for our education system, a student today would be much better off (per the old saying) sitting on a log in the forest with a good teacher.

We hear a lot about FIRSTS! First this & first that. As a syndicated writer I get two books a week in the mail, labeled "first on the subject," "first to tell it like it is," etc. Most are old-hat, *thirty*-first.

Harry's absorbing new book *On Re-Making the World* is *really* a first. And Harry is used to being first not only in content, but readability. Congratulations, Harry!

Tom Anderson
one-time candidate for US presidency
publisher American Way Features
    news syndicate
author Straight Talk newsletter
Pigeon Forge, Tennessee

As I see this volume...

H arry Schultz has consistently been a pioneer, ahead of his time in floating new ideas which may at first seem outlandish and impossible, but which very often, over time, become mainstream thinking.

For example, Sir Harry was one of the very first to articulate the case for U.S. aid to anti-Communist freedom fighters as a low-cost means of challenging the Soviet empire and advancing the cause of human liberty. He was pushing for Jonas Savimbi in Angola, the Contras in Nicaragua, RENAMO in Mozambique, and the mujahideen in Afghanistan long before the so-called "Reagan Doctrine" was conceived and initiated.

Now Harry is at it again. In his provocative new book, he makes the case for redefining national boundaries in order to accommodate ethnic, religious, and cultural coherence, rather than the sometimes artificial designs of geo-political mapmakers.

One need not endorse each detail of Harry Schultz's grand design to accept his premise that self-determination very often requires the breakup of empires, large and small, rather than their expansion.

Certainly, this is a thesis which will be welcomed by peoples as diverse as the Kurds, the Croats, the Slovaks, the Rehoboth Basters in Namibia, the Eritreans in Ethiopia, and, of course, the various peoples held captive within the confines of the decaying, corrupt, yet still powerful USSR.

It has long been agreed that accountability is a prerequisite to liberty in any politicized society. Harry makes the point that localism is an essential ingredient if accountability is to be achieved and maintained, whether the issue is crime, education, taxes, or charity.

In 1813, Thomas Jefferson told John Adams that "the issue today is the same as it has been throughout all history, whether man shall be allowed to govern himself or be ruled by a small elite."

Jefferson's insight is still valid. George Bush's vision of a New World Order is but the latest manifestation of an imperial dream which has plagued mankind throughout history.

There is a constant tension between the desires of individuals and families, on the one hand, to be self-governing and independent, and on the other, for power-seeking politicizers and greed-oriented commercialists to feed their egos and enhance their personal power by confiscating the rights of others.

Read Harry's book. It will get you thinking. It may even start a trend.

Howard Phillips
President, Conservative Caucus
Vienna, Virginia, USA

From the Leading US Think Tank, A Comment on This Book

From Yugoslavia and the USSR to India and southern Africa, the empires of old are crumbling and the politicians of the world cannot stop it. Harry Schultz asks the logical question: Why is big better? Why shouldn't we encourage these breakups?

In the US we have learned that "economies of scale" may work in certain industries, but politically "big" puts the individual at a disadvantage.

The US federal system (now honored more in the breach than in the observance) was the answer of the Founding Fathers to this challenge. If it can be reinvigorated, it may still prove the answer for us in the US.

But for many, both in the US and around the world, the Schultz concept of mini-states is one we should debate and develop.

When I read Harry's analysis for the first time, I certainly didn't want to agree with all of it. But he has made me realize that the freest, safest and some of the most successful and enjoyable times of my life—for both business and pleasure—have been in small nations such as Hong Kong, Singapore, Taiwan and Liechtenstein.

In fact, Liechtenstein, from its efficient and manageable capital city of Vaduz; to the pastoral town of Bendern, to the industrial suburb of Schaun, and in the mountain village of Malbun, has it all: honest and small government; efficient public services; beautiful art treasures and fine cultural activities; and a thriving entrepreneurial class which is encouraged and not discouraged by the government. And all this with only 25,000 citizens. Too bad we can't all become Liechtensteiners; but then Liechtenstein wouldn't be Liechtenstein anymore!

So, join Harry as he examines how we might encourage new Liechtensteins and new Hong Kongs to come into being.

Harry doesn't claim to have all the answers. For example, what do we do about defense? But like the HSL newsletter which we count on to cut through so much official fog and disinformation, Harry asks the right questions and expands the range of options for all of us. I hope you will find Re-making the World as provocative and stimulating as I have.

Edwin J. Feulner, Jr., Ph.D.
President, Heritage Foundation
Washington, DC 20002

Chapter 1

And the Premise is—

T hat: Big landmass nations, like the US, Canada, Brazil, the USSR, China, Australia, Sudan, Angola, Ethiopia, & Chad, should be broken up into *several smaller countries* (even some smaller nations have some bits that can be broken off to the profound advantage of all).

The reasons are impressive, in our opinion.

For a start, it would end or drastically reduce the killing now going on due to ethnic rivalries; people generally can have far more voice in their govt. & suffer less bureaucracy if their country is relatively small. Individual freedom would increase in the US, in the USSR, in China, etc., if they were cut up into several nations.

That *govt. itself* should be small is a separate (& important) question, which we'll touch on in passing here & there & in our conclusion. But that is NOT the premise of this book, which deals basically in the physical size of nations, & the redrawing of borders to match up with religions, cultures, races, economics, topography.

Civil War a Mistake?

How can anyone, in unemotional retrospect, defend the US civil war? Can you defend the loss of hundreds of thousands of people JUST so that people could say "we are ONE nation," a UNION? What's so wonderful about the union? Any union. What's wrong with two nations?

What difference would it honestly have made if there had been a North & South USA instead of one oversized giant of a country? Was it worth the life of even ONE person, to be killed so that Abe Lincoln could make speeches about his precious union? But in fact *600,000* were slaughtered, and a *million* wounded, just so there could be one flag flying over the USA instead of two flags?

(These civil war statistics are from a Spring 1991 US 10-hour TV documentary which was researched deeper than prior estimates.)

Since the 1800s began, the US expanded its territory & its population until it is now ungovernable. The choking debt is one indication of that. Runaway crime rates are another. So are drugs. And alcoholism.

Should Texas have been given the chance to be a country, as it wanted? Why in heavens not? It may not be too late! We'll examine that in another chapter. (I conducted a poll on the subject; it's fascinating!)

You've heard that the GNP of California is bigger than most nations in the UN. A few have dared to say: "California should be a country of itself." We will dare to discuss it later on.

If you had a country the size of a village, you can readily see that everyone could have some voice in local affairs; everyone could know what's going on, cope with local charitable needs without middle men, easily embarrass any teenager intent on drugs, & local leaders would be readily accountable to their next-door neighbors for taxes & overly severe laws & miscarriages of justice. Accountability & responsibility are wonderful bi-products of small political units.

In colonial days, the wooden "stocks" (with head & hands protruding through holes) were sufficient **embarrassment** to stop crime from spreading. In a village, that is first class *crime prevention*. As a country grows, this disintegrates into "prison systems" which encourages/breeds far far more crime than it deters.

But when a nation's capital is 2,000 miles away, the accountability factor goes out the window. A Congressman must serve perhaps a half million or maybe 5 million people. He can't possibly know all his constituents, nor could they meet him.

The interests of people in one corner of the USSR or the USA or China are vastly different from those in another corner. Far better they each manage their own local affairs, *totally.*

Lives are being lost today, as I write, to resolve boundary disputes in many parts of the world, from the Baltic states to the Soviet nation state of Georgia, from the Basques area of Spain to the north of Ethiopia. Not to forget the Kurds who have been fighting & dying for decades to get some control over their lives. Why? Why should people have to die or risk death to have their views taken into consideration? Especially as all it takes is a different *perspective* on "borders."

Importantly, why should a govt. kill people with govt. troops who seek to get independence or even merely local autonomy? The concept that the "whole" of every country must be preserved as though it were some **supreme** & moral prerogative, is invalid. There is no *compelling logic* in that concept.

This book is what you might call a prototype, with a sequel to follow with more details, ideas, feedback from readers, updating of subsequent events. In fact, we may do an *annual* sequel because this is a watershed volume, that separates old-fashioned BIGness, union, centralization thinking in politics & geo-politics from what I fervently hope will be a new generation of thought for smallness, de-centralization, greater freedom, more voice, more influence for the individual—which has been LOST in the growth of the nation state & the amalgamations & territorial acquisitions.

The USSR once consisted only of Russia. Subsequently it gobbled up a lot of other nations & became the USSR (to a degree the USA was created in almost the same way). Now most of the gobbled people want their independence back. The big USSR turned out to be a dud idea, which reduced everyone to the lowest common denominator, i.e., a low standard. (Communism & socialism don't redistribute wealth; they equalize poverty.)

By virtue of their size, unfortunately, all big nations do that to their citizens. Big nations reduce potentially big people into small people. Instead of being treated as an individual, you are treated more like a number because through sheer size, anything else becomes harder to manage. (The giants of the past appear nowhere, or much less often, in recent history.) Individualism is disappearing, is even being **discouraged** in some places! E.g., China & the US state education system.

If big was great, school classes should be 100 students per class. But you know very well that classes of 20-30 are better, & where possible 5-10 are wonderfully better still.

And if, as I have come to believe, education is the best (only?) hope for civilization to stop killing itself off, with endless violence, then education is best promoted in smaller nations.

Look at the literacy rate in the small nations of Europe, versus the low rate in the big nations of Brazil, USSR, India, China. I know you can find exceptions to this & in fact to every premise, but the exceptions tend to prove the rule.

A bi-product of giving the chop to big nations is that it will *revitalize* both sectors, for each will get a positive jolt, feeling of greater equity, more chance for justice, and more opportunity, etc.

Think for example how people in Quebec will feel when they are suddenly a country, not just a province. The atmosphere will be electric. And happy.

How will all this chop-chop come about? The answer is: NOT out of the barrel of a gun. That is savagery. The answer must be: by people's *referendum voting.* If people in the big countries start petitions, they can force the issue, get a referendum that is either legally binding or morally influential on their govt.

Perhaps we can even get some brave humanoid to propose to the UN that referendums be held in every nation to determine if their citizens prefer a reshaping of their nations for the greater good. It would be voluntary of course, but it could have much moral persuasion.

It'll take time, but the HOPE that will be kindled by the start of the process will STOP much current violence. If people can look forward to the possible or probable success of a redrawing of boundaries & recasting of nations, it will spark great enthusiasm & new planning.

If we can get the big-name syndicated columnists to discuss the idea, pro & con, a momentum can be built. I hope every talk-show host in the world wants to interview me or one of my team, to put this idea in front of everyone's nose. I can see the columnists' headlines now: "Trim the World?" And: "Big is Bureaucratic?" or "Big is Clumsy?" or "Tiny is Terrific!" or "Cutting Nations Down to Size." Maybe even: "Takeaway Countries."

We don't mind humor along with serious thinking. It's all grist for the mill. In the end, it may save millions of lives. And create rich fulfillment. End decades/centuries of frustration.

Pragmatically, it will create thousands of new jobs. Each new country will need new money to be printed, new stamps, new passports, new capital cities, new govt. facilities, new political jobs. And if most of this is done via the private sector, there will be a sharp *reduction of taxes* all round. A private postal system can cut current postal costs by 30-50%. Roads can also be privatized, & certainly education can and should be.

Free enterprise can provide MORE & better service for LESS cost! That is not the message of this volume & I must not be tempted to dwell too much on that aspect to the detriment of the main message. Yet it would be foolish to say nothing, for creating new countries to be run by socialistic or welfare state methods would be inefficient & a wasted opportunity.

Small is Something Special. And *Privatization Produces Perfection.* Well, as perfect as you can get in this very imperfect world. The combination of smallness and privatization is nationhood at its best. Hong Kong is an example of a very small state with very little govt. interference, that churns out more GNP than any place of comparable size on earth.

History has brutalized geo-political boundaries. The world is divided illogically and it is up to us to re-organize the geo-political nightmare thrown upon us by our predecessors/ancestors. Ambitious empires have expanded & then imploded, all the while wreaking havoc on the world's borders and people.

Chapter 2

Examples from round the world

This isn't so much a chapter as an explanation of how *widespread* the need is for trimming many countries down to a more manageable/productive/constructive/democratic size.

Also, the **reasons** for dividing certain nations up are not just to be more manageable, though one can make a case for that easily enough, but to give a voice to groups who don't have proper (or any) representation, to stop **bloodshed** where there is currently fighting/killing in order to win sovereignty where they are now ruled by people they consider outsiders (like the Kurds feel about the Iraqis).

It is also to *lower taxes,* improve the quality of govt., bring welfare supervision to the *community* level instead of the federal level, bring down crime & drug rates, & improve education (so that there's some hope for the future.

In my view, morality itself will improve with smaller nations.

To some degree, one can use the old example of what happens in an office or shop when the boss goes away. The mice will play when the cat is away. With the capital city 1,000 or 2,000 or 6,000 miles away, there is a lesser feeling of responsibility or cohesion. Orders that come from a distant capital are less respected, a kind of govt. by remote control, management by strangers.

Conversely a nearly ideal community seemed to exist in former New England (USA) days where the town hall gave everyone a chance to SEE what was happening, to speak up if they wished, to be a part of the whole.

Switzerland is perhaps the "best" overall nation in the world today. Yet it has few natural resources, very little flat land for agriculture & is divided by people who speak 4 languages in each of its 4 sectors. Yet it works "like a Swiss watch" without violence & with more referendums per head than any country on earth. The referendi seems one key to Swiss success.

The size of Switzerland is perhaps nearly ideal. The smallness hasn't presented any military risk. They have, in fact, the largest army in Europe! What? Yes, because each male is in the army reserves, though he works in offices, etc. He undergoes annual training in the army.

Some people would argue that splitting up big nations into small ones creates a military risk. Not only does the Swiss example refute that but apart from the Swiss, not every nation *needs* a big army. The solution is to have a military assistance pact with friendly neighbors.

If the US were chopped up, each segment would make defense treaties with all or most of the other segments. The (let's say) six North American countries would probably fight any major war as allies, as a very cohesive unit, just as the US of today has fought wars with other allies throughout its history. But if one segment didn't want to join the others, they could agree not to take part in some war, like Panama (1989) or the Gulf (1991), if they choose.

In Chapter 5, we'll discuss the possible "new face" map of North America.

But before we get to it, let's talk *principles*, in chapters 3 & 4. Let me also differentiate between two groups of countries. First example are those nations where despots rule & the people merely want the despot overthrown. These people don't want autonomy per se. They simply want a vote. They want democracy. Borders are not involved.

This book is *not* basically concerned with that problem. (Although a book is currently in the works written by someone I know well, that gives advice, for the first time in book form, on how to overthrow a dictatorship. The name of this brave new book is "*The Self-Determination Handbook.*" Watch for it. It'll be hard to find as bookstores won't likely handle it. Watch or write to my news-letter for the details in late 1991. PO Box 622, CH-1001 Lausanne, Switzerland.

In this book we're concerned with a second group of countries, where in most cases the country was put together wrongly at the start, through arbitrary boundaries (like Sudan and Ethiopia), or, countries taken over, i.e., won through war (like Manchuria), or, where demographics changed so the population mix is no longer served by the present structure (like Spain), or countries just grew "like topsy" (e.g., US & Canada) & they don't any longer fully satisfy the original intentions for it.

Original US Intentions

For example, the USA started life as 13 colonies. They had the world's best Constitution ever written to that date, or since. It provided for 13 separate, independent states with many nationalistic rights. Most decisions were to be made within each colony (state) & the federal govt. was intentionally a weak landlord with minor powers.

Even currency was not issued by the federal govt., but by individual banks scattered around the colonies. Postage stamps were separate for a while. There were no passports. There was great *individual* freedom, probably more than at any time before in at least modern history.

That individual freedom reached its modern-day pinnacle in the US (& subsequently for the whole free world) around 1900, give or take 7 years. Then it was all downhill. It coincided, not by accident, with the gradual loss of power by the separate states & the gaining of power by the federal government.

The US became less free as it expanded from 13 small colonies to gobble up the Louisiana purchase, California, Texas, Alaska, Hawaii.

But the steepest loss of freedom didn't occur until the income tax was created & with the formation of the Federal Reserve both between 1900 & 1915.

That loss escalated under Franklin D. Roosevelt, then slowed down, but speeded up after World War II when the US government decided it was smarter than the free market, so it would determine exactly how business would run. Washington set interest rates, & fed money into the banking system it created, or withdrew it, at its whim.

This is not a book about the loss of *individual* freedom in the world, but it's clear to a history student that as governments around the world followed the awful Roosevelt example & began controlling the business life of their countries, that they would increasingly & automatically (if not intentionally) control the lives of each citizen.

You must forgive a battered old freedom fighter for adding a little of this freedom spice to a book that is basically on a different subject.

In the chapters ahead I divide the world into grapefruit segments & dissect each one, ferreting out specific examples of how we can dramatically improve life on this planet by re-adjusting our territorial imperatives!

If **private property** is the key (as it is) to free markets & the free world & democracy, then would you agree that having badly structured nations & boundaries can upset the emotions & reduce or destroy incentives of a lot of people? If so, we had better examine how we can straighten out this slipped disc, this spine out of adjustment—that runs down the back of so many nations.

The most flagrant need for breaking up big countries is the Soviet Union, currently referred to by many as the **Soviet Disunion**. We'll deal with that in a later chapter, but if you agree that the USSR should be disassembled, then I hope you will be objective when we talk about the same kind of re-juggling of places you know better, like Canada & the US. Please try to be unemotional as we deal with countries in a way that may occasionally seem rather cold-blooded.

But patriotism is really a much misunderstood word & concept. Should one be patriotic to a particular piece of real estate? Were the US founding fathers that way? Hardly! They were patriotic only to the IDEALS they put forth in the Bill of Rights & the Constitution. These checks & balances had meaning & protection. The dirt under their feet had none.

So please let us look at these matters without emotion. Just as a passport should be looked at like a bus ticket (not part of the flag), so should boundaries be viewed as lines in sand, not in concrete. Borders have *been changing* since life began forming into communities on earth. They will **keep on** changing, whether we like it or not. Why not harmonize it?

Animals & fish have boundaries too, very real ones. They do it via instinct. We have lost the edge from our cave man instincts. We substituted brute force & have brought awful burdens on millions of fellow earth-dwellers.

What I'm saying is: for a big change, for heaven's sake, let's do some intelligent PLANNING for the next changes, instead of just letting them **happen**. Let's stop being the *victim* of boundaries, & instead be like some wise men of ancient times who set forth as few rules as possible & who would seek the council of every woman & man before taking any action, especially regarding the boundaries of the place we live.

Isn't it about time?

Finally, may I point to the British empire (among others) as a positive example of a single BIG country (which the empire was, in effect) which was saved by its own dissolution, its dismemberment. They broke up the empire & created instead The Commonwealth. Separate units, but working together.

I can envision the present-day USA becoming the Commonwealth of the USA. Or perhaps Canada & US becoming the Commonwealth of North America. Separate & equal. Some 7 or 8 different nations of North America working together in peace, harmony & prosperity, each enjoying to the full the fruits of their separate cultures.

Now before we take a look at North America, in Chapter 6, where we start to take the world under our microscope, a continent at a time, let's discuss the ideal size of a country, principles & responsibilities in chapters 3 & 4.

You'll notice different *writing styles* in this book, because my research editors Gordon Frisch & Anton Keller contributed certain pages which I have left largely untouched, to introduce different perspectives on the overall subject matter of this book. One writes in the style of a scientist, the other academically, which is what they are. E.g., you'll note Anton Keller's Swiss Germanic style in parts of chapters 3, 4, 11, 13, 15 & half of 8. Gordon's style appears in chapters 9, 10, & 14.

Some people may nickname this book: *Chop Chop*, & I don't mind because it implies the kind of pruning we will do to our nations' fruit trees & rose bushes. We will make some strategic cutting, chopping the old out-of-control withering or stagnant branches. Through prudent pruning will come forth new life, growth, new "roses." All made possible through our enlightened chopping.

With the daily headlines screaming about cries for separation by Yugoslavia, the Baltics, Africa, certain Soviet states, & such, time is running out, in my opinion, for applying some new-fashioned remedies to these **desperate** cries for help. Let's have some new thinking—to save lives, foster fresh incentives & cure mal-representation. It's truly urgent!

Chapter 3

On the Ideal Size of Nations

Some Frank Speaking on an Overdue Return to Citizen-States

Make no mistake about it: the breakup of nations is *no calamity*. It is always an opportunity; but its *suppression* may lead to calamities—just like some medicine is worse than the illness, and some measures to fight ecological disasters do more harm than good. For a nation's evolution and devolution, its constitution, dissolution, reconstitution and fusion are no less *natural* processes than seasonal growth, the blossoming, the crumbling and the eventual decomposing of flowers, leaves and other signs of nature.

There is a quantitative time-scale difference, say from under one year to a few hundred years. This is influenced and determined by both external and internal factors, by dynamic forces outside a nation's control, and also by home-made growth, stability and/or disintegration.

Political borders reflect *static factors*, such as geography (mountains, rivers), natural resources (oil, water, rainfall, soil fertility), climate, etc. Yet, as testimony to endless power shifts in mankind's history, they continue to be subject to *dynamic factors*, such as the economic and political fortunes and ambitions of people and their leaders, their education, ethnic roots, religion, nationalities, laws, and resultant conflicts within their societies and/or with neighbors.

What we see unfolding in and around the USSR, the Near East (Kurds, Palestinians, Cypriots) and the Far East should surprise nobody. Nor frighten us either—provided those concerned will recognize and understand the forces underlying these developments and provided they'll wisely accommodate and channel them. What is needed, is more imagination and flexibility to accommodate the unsuppressible factors which indicate redrawing political borders to genuinely reflect humanity's social, economic, political, ethnic and cultural evolution.

Here are some thoughts on these forces and their interplay. A stock-taking on *what a viable nation needs.* And some reflections on possible *paths to get there—or get lost.*

Where Did We Come From, Where Do We Stand, and Where Do We Go?

"At a minimum," columnist Jim Hoagland recently wrote,[1] Iraq, Yugoslavia, and the Soviet Union (and he might have added: Quebec, Corsica, Basque-Catalonia, Flanders, Scotland, South Tyrol and, yes, even Geneva) are synonyms for nationality crises which "force the world to rethink the *automatic allegiance* to 'territorial integrity' that national governments have pledged since World War II as a way to avoid wars and avoid responsibility for each other's problems."

Jonathan Eyal[2] followed up with a lucid demonstration on how "the Western notion of the nation-state as the only viable and desirable political unit, created havoc in the Balkans. …The maintenance of Yugoslavia (or similar outgrowths) as one nation under *Serbian* domination (or some other) will ultimately be more destabilizing than the country's disintegration."

Indeed, while the history of the Serbs[3] was seen already in 1919 to be "complex beyond ordinary complexity, and bloody beyond ordinary bloodiness," the past, present and future history of Americans, Indians, Hungarians, Balts, Swiss, Turks, Kurds, Palestinians

---

[1] *"Union versus Separation: Apart Can be Better,"* Washington Post/International Herald Tribune, May 9, 1991

[2] *"Balkan states crack on rock of reality,"* The Guardian, May 10, 1991

[3] Harold Temperlay, *History of Serbia,* 1919: The Guardian, 5/10/91

and any other People deserving this distinction is basically not much different. Mostly, it is a fair reflection of its members' and its leaders' ability—or *lack* thereof:

a) to *adapt* to constantly changing circumstances,

b) to recognize and realize *opportunities* for strengthening or improving their lot as compared to other people competing for the available places under the sun, and

c) to play ball in line with the *evolving rules*.

Thus if the self-serving chancelleries of Western Europe, under British[4] or other leadership, succeeded in stampeding the European Community into some sort of "life-preserving" intervention in Yugoslavia it might benefit Yugoslavia's republics and people less than it would *strengthen* the bureaucrats and their institutions in Brussels, as was the case when the USSR helped quell national aspirations under Tito. Given the *historically inescapable fate of suppressive structures and their auxiliaries*—with the Soviet Union as a case study—this would not exactly bode well for the EC (Euro. Common Mkt.)

The problem of national awakening, of humanity's long-suppressed legitimate aspirations, goes much deeper. It leads straight to the question of the *legitimacy of our leaders*. The reason being that even in Switzerland, where voters are invited to cast their ballots at least four times every year on communal, cantonal and national questions, the citizen, increasingly, takes a bath.

In the face of his creeping castration by growing regulations and criminalization of the market, by a judicial system that protects the authorities not the individual, and by unwittingly favoring private and public bureaucracies, he sees himself ever more sheep-like

---

[4] The Guardian reported May 19, 1991, that Britain's Foreign Secretary, Douglas Hurd, urged "the European Community to offer to conciliate between Yugoslavia's warring republics, to avert the break-up of the country. ... Britain would be ready to support Yugoslavia's transformation into a loose confederation, but is strongly opposed to secession by Croatia, Slovenia or any of the other republics. ... [Mr. Hurd tried] to persuade the EC to issue a statement supporting continuation of Yugoslavia as an entity." The Guardian thus editorialized "The West... fears the implications for its backing of Gorbachev against the independence movements in the Soviet Union. It even fears the implications in its own back yards—in Scotland, Catalonia, Corsica."

with the *ARIGIN* syndrome, i.e., official ARrogance, IGnorance and INcompetence dominating the political *and* the private economic landscape.

We live in an era of *information saturation.* Thereby the fundamental requirements of a democracy anywhere (and even more so in a direct democracy like Switzerland) are less and less met.

Increasingly lacking are the citizens' public spirit, their capacity to grasp complex problems affecting society and their relations with the outside world, and their willingness to take risks and share responsibility.

The net result is *government by saturation,* i.e., exclusive attendance to matters aired only by the mass media. This presupposes that these information channels have a monopoly for good ideas. *Governments are thus operating below their task levels—and thus with reduced legitimacy.*

Where does that lead us? Perhaps democracy is too demanding a form of government for many people in this world? Or is it simply not sufficiently understood by those who favor it without recognizing its fundamental incompatibility with the *upside-down citizen-state relationship we can see all around us?*

Thus, we have defined what we must aim for. Namely *first,* the reanimation of the citizen, the responsible, risk-taking and enterprising *homo oeconomicus,* so that he (and not the "public servants" to which he has so far had to submit) may again take charge as the only *true sovereign* in his country. This requires *re-introducing the right to UNDISCLOSED private property,* as well as *cutting* the umbilical cord between the citizen and the state, i.e., his obligation to take down his trousers before the taxman by producing his income-records to *prove* what he *declared* (via his signature) to *be* his income.

This requires an educational effort that starts at home and spreads to schools and universities, now a nest of ignorance and conformity.

All of which requires a built-in incentive for *mobility* beyond one's cultural horizon, such as may be provided by an *Atlanticpass* available to American, Canadian and European citizens on the basis of existing—but mostly forgotten—bilateral friendship, commerce and establishment treaties.[5] Moreover, a genuine catalyst for building a viable, confederated Europe might be created in the form of a *Europass*. It could guarantee Europe-wide freedom of movement, establishment and exercise of profession, and would be issued to all citizens of member countries of the Council of Europe.[6]

And *second*, the setting of those political conditions which will provide the fertile terrain for such grown-up citizens to do their thing, prosper and find happiness for themselves, their family and the community they discovered to fit them best. This political frame may be *defined* as follows:

> A nation, ideally, extends over the territory within which the citizens' duly elected and effectively accountable authorities are ready, willing and able to provide for its residents' free and responsible pursuit of happiness— notably to genuinely protect them against foreign physical or economic harm, such as fiscal and administrative transgressions under whatever title that might be.

To be sure, *there is no permanent ideal size of a nation,* and the leaders of even the longest enduring nations, such as the Swiss Confederation, risk losing the family silver and put the national existence at risk if they fail to adequately attend to the *qualitative factors* which make up a nation and which provide for its continuity. Small can indeed be beautiful. Small nations are indeed usually more governable. And competently governed small nations are more likely to

---

[5] For recent lucid accounts of the cultural *and* economic net benefit of immigrants to their host societies, see also: Julian Simon, *"Europe's Costly Immigration Myths,"* The Wall Street Journal Europe, April 18, 1991; *"Yes, they'll fit in too,"* The Economist, May 11, 1991. Some skeptics may be reminded that Switzerland, in the last century, was essentially an underdeveloped agriculture-oriented society whose transformation into one of the world's most sophisticated commercial and industrial societies is largely due to the enterprising immigrants it let in freely notably until 1914.

[6] Each member of the European Assembly has the right to formally set things in motion to this effect—as, in theory, has each Member of the Council's governing Council of Ministers. Any takers?

withstand the hurricanes of history and to prosper in rapidly changing circumstances. They tend to be more flexible. But by and for
itself, *smallness is no guarantee of virtue—just as bigness is no shield against
failure.* The competence & morality of its citizens, their ideals, and
their leaders makes part of the difference. The structure, standards
& laws are another part. Size is another part.

To illustrate this more bluntly: If not for reasons of geo-political
imperatives and other earthy interests of other members of the family of nations, *Kuwait* would not—and should not—have been *spared*
the destiny into which their leaders had driven them. And if it were
not for such Soviet leaders as Eduard Shevardnadze (who was
Georgia's Communist party chief) whose behavior seemingly demon-
strates willingness to do their utmost in addressing root causes of
Soviet society's present miseries, the people of the free world would
(rightly) not given any moral or hard-currency credit to the remnants
of a discredited and future-less power structure.

Indeed, that would be ill-advised and do no *real* good to the
people still vegetating under these Soviet structures if that help
contributed to their maintenance, including the use of force by the
disintegrating USSR.

Yet, all this doesn't mean there are *no* opportunities to help these
people and their leaders—provided they demonstrate, with words,
actions and inactions, that they are genuinely interested in viable
ways out of the mess they inherited or contributed to.

It will be up to these people and their leaders to decide whether
and under what conditions all this eventually will lead to the *con-
solidation* or the total *break-up* of states which are held together with
difficulty and no clear purpose or viable unifying theme. And
whether the final structures can and will be molded into dignified,
recognized and viable members of the family of nations. All data
and ideas compiled in this book are aimed, and may be put to good
use in this direction—even though we have no illusions as to the
real world.

Indeed, the not-invented-here and the ARIGIN syndrome in
high places, i.e., the critical mass of arrogance, ignorance and incom-

petence, are quite human and thus omni-present phenomena. Yet, it should be noted that this is a sure-fire recipe for failure *anywhere*, for *any* nation, be it big or small. The forces of nature/history have a way of catching up with societies who have lost their moral rootings, whose corruption and decadence has become an insult to human beings everywhere, and whose only real power of conviction is the power of the gun or the power to bribe.

All this leads to fundamental questions concerning the existence of man, his role and the relations between him, his society and the State whose passport he carries. Although not apparently linked to the objective set out in the title of this book, the pursuit of these questions and the development of answers to them may be found to be insightful on that very question of the ideal size of a nation. That view will become apparent upon reading extracts of *Centesimus Annus*, the Encyclica Pope John Paul II gave us recently.

Chapter 4

Principles to Remember on Responsibilities of the Individual and National Landholdings

The saying goes that *an individual may claim the land* (1) which he can encompass within one day's horse ride; (2) which his family's labors can bring to fruit; and (3) which he is willing and capable to effectively defend.

By analogy, *a nation's founding fathers (or their successors) may not want to stake (or maintain) their border posts* (1) beyond the limits of their means for harmonious development; (2) beyond their citizens' effective interests and capacities; or (3) beyond the limits of their nationally available means for effective control and defense.

We do not advocate further territorial sales, such as happened in the notorious cases of Alaska and Louisiana. But we *question the wisdom* of *unifying* into a federated system of diverse people with incompatible backgrounds, whether the USSR or the USA. And it definitely speaks *against* proceeding with the *present* Orwellian, over-bureaucratized hobo stew cooked up, in Brussels' EC (common mkt.), Tower of Babel, for some 24 still independent European countries.

Furthermore, these principles invite hope of *alternatives* for home-grown long-term solutions which could become socially, economically and politically more desirable for regional stability and prosperity. To this end, the *Hong Kong example of a 99-year territorial lease offers food for thought.*

Perhaps Messrs. Yeltsin and Kaifu might find happiness for their people with an agreement for a long-term lease of the *Kurile islands* to the Russian Federation—in return for leasing to Japan a *continental settlement zone* facing the Pacific (which could provide badly needed development impulses to the Russian Federation, and could offer the Japanese people a well-prepared refuge zone whenever a long-anticipated earthquake strikes its islands).

The countries making up Kurdistan are dependent on the Euphrates and the Tigris rivers. They might find it advantageous to entrust the Kurds with guarding the water and to jointly lease to them these traditionally Kurdish areas. In the case of the *Palestinians,* a similar solution (e.g., involving Jordan or Southern Iraq) may provide for early statehood of this people, too—independent of the fate of current Mid-Eastern hagglings which pass as preliminary peace negotiations.

The Baltic problem might also be solved in this way. The USSR, while it lasts, might conclude a long-term lease agreement with each of the three Baltic States, thus allowing them to rejoin the family of nations and be recognized as independent states and trading partners. Any successor to the present USSR, in international law and for all practical purposes, could not lay any claim on any of the Baltic states. For not only has the USSR's claim to them never been supported in international law, but its likely successor—i.e., an eventual *confederation* embracing *some* of the USSR's republics—is most unlikely to disregard the disastrous failure of 70 years of crass mismanagement and forced national unity.

Basically, we are looking for applications of a time-tested, yet unpracticed method for the *indirect analysis and resolution of complex problems.* Example: See nearby graphic, posing the problem of *linking all nine points with only four straight lines drawn,* without taking the pen off the paper. You can see that *within* the confines of the *apparent* elements—i.e., the square delineated by the 9 points—the problem is seemingly unsolvable as it takes 5 lines. *As is the case with many problems, only by breaking out of apparent confines can a problem be solved— and elegantly at that.*

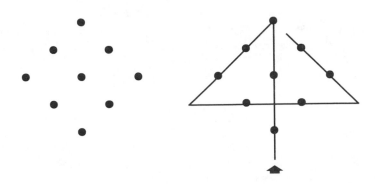

Similarly assistance can be expected via diplomatic support, from foreign leaders' goodwill, such as may continue to be tapped by the rising new leaders, particularly in Russia, Lithuania, Georgia and Ukraine. Which brings us to an *almost forgotten but potentially fruitful loose end of Europe's colorful history.* Reference is made to the *Memelland,* the 1,100 square-mile northern sliver of East Prussia (located along the internationalized Niemen river and embracing the Baltic port of Klaipeda).

Founded in the 13th century as Neu-Dort-mund by German settlers, it had been part of East Prussia until 1945, except in the years 1923-1939. *In theory,* this piece of land is governed by a never-abrogated, and thus readily revivable treaty, i.e., the 1924 Memel Convention, which involved United States rights and is signed by: France, Great Britain, Italy, Japan and Lithuania. *In practice,* Stalin united it in 1945 with the Lithuanian Soviet Socialist Republic.

Significantly, the signatories of this other forgotten treaty thus provided for the transfer to Lithuania of

all rights and titles ceded to them (art.1).

But they also determined:

Rights of sovereignty over the Memel Territory or the exercise of such rights may not be transferred without the consent of the High Contracting Parties. (art.15)

And under present circumstances particularly interesting to all parties concerned are these provisions of the Convention's integral *Statute of the Memel Territory*[7]:

> The Harbour Board shall maintain the existing free zone and provide such extensions as the transit traffic may warrant, either by extending the present zone or by the creation of a new one. In the latter event, the existing zone may be abolished if in such new free zone the traffic can be adequately dealt with. (Annex, art.13)

Thus, the Baltic debate might benefit from the perspective of looking beyond present conditions. The *secret protocols* of the *Molotov-Ribbentrop Pact of 1939*[8], the 1926 Non-Aggression Treaty, (& amendments), and other agreements between Lithuania and the USSR are not the only relevant international law references. The *Lithuanian*[9]

---

[7] Other noteworthy *Statute* provisions include:

> The port of Memel shall be considered as a port of international concern. The recommendations adopted by the Barcelona Conference concerning ports subject to an international regime shall be applied thereto, unless otherwise herein provided. (art.2)

> There shall be a Harbour Board, which shall consist of three members appointed for three years and eligible for reappointment, as follows:
> 1) one representing Lithuanian economic interests, to be appointed by the Lithuanian Government;
> 2) one representing the economic interests of the Memel Territory, to be appointed by the Directorate of the Territory;
> 3) one to be appointed by the Chairman of the Advisory and Technical Committee for Communications and Transit of the League of Nations. This member shall not be a citizen of a Niemen riparian State. He shall give special attention to international economic interests served by the port and particularly to those of the districts for which the port of Memel is the natural outlet. (art.5)

[8] Helmut Konig, *"Das deutsch-sowjetische Vertragswerk von 1939 und seine Geheimen Zusatzprotokolle. Eine Dokumentation,"* Osteuropa, May 1989.

[9] Only an again *truly independent Lithuania* may be internationally recognized as the legitimate holder of all titles attributed to Lithuania under the 1924 Memel Convention. However, as such it would also be subject to the related legal consequences, e.g., the ruling handed down by the *Permanent Court of International Justice* in The Hague which, on August 8, 1932, concluded that "le Statut de Memel doit etre tenue pour un arrangement de nature conventionelle, liant la Lithuanie" (CPJI, 1932, p.300).

and third party rights and obligations emanating from the 1924 Memel Convention, in the hands of visionary and competent politicians, might help resolve some regional issues. Belatedly rediscovering and honoring this formal treaty might facilitate economic progress based on democracy, enterprising citizens and the rule of law. This would meet vital economic and political interests of all concerned.

An *International Baltic Conference* could be called by the Soviet leadership (or others). It might involve France, Germany, UK, Italy, Japan, Lithuania and the USA as parties to the Memel Convention. And it might thus effectively draw on the goodwill some Soviet leaders enjoy among Western politicians.

Conceivably, both the Memel Territory and the present Kaliningrad Oblast, with the help of Western and Arab investments and Soviet Jews emigrating there—could be turned into a viable *Baltic Hong Kong*. As a treaty-based international center contributing to regional stability, prosperity and security,[10] linked to a Russian— and why not, a European—Commonwealth inspiring full confidence and radiating mutually beneficial cultural, political and commercial impulses in all directions.

---

[10] As to this zone's security status, its creators might find inspirations in the time-tested Swiss neutrality formula, devised by the French-Genevese diplomat Charles Pictet-de Rochemont and adopted at the Paris Congress on November 20, 1815, by the Representatives of Austria, France, Great Britain, Prussia, Russia, a.o.:

The neutrality and inviolability of Switzerland and its independence of all foreign influences are in the true interests of the politique of Europe as a whole. (CPJI, 1930, C, 17-1, II, p.1191)

Chapter 5

Case by Case—First the USA

*"The Gettysburg Address is poetry, not logic; beauty, not sense. Think of the argument in it. Put it into the cold words of everyday. The doctrine is simply this: that the Union soldiers who died at Gettysburg sacrificed their lives to the cause of self-determination— 'that government of the people, by the people, for the people' should not perish from the earth. It is difficult to imagine anything more untrue. The Union soldiers in that battle actually fought **against** self-determination; it was the Confederates who fought for the right of their people to govern themselves. What was the practical effect of the battle of Gettysburg? What else than the destruction of the old sovereignty of the states, i.e., of the people of the states?"*

—H. L. Mencken

This will probably be the most contentious chapter in this book, so I'm starting the case by case list with it rather than taking all the easy & obvious examples first.

For openers, I think there was no justification for killing hundreds of thousands of citizens in the Civil War in order to obtain unanimity. There was no desperate "Need" of a union. Separate nations would have been as good if not better. If the North couldn't understand that, there should have been a general ballot to let the people decide, not a general war.

The Constitution stipulated a country run of, for, and by the *people*, not the preferences of rail splitter Abe Lincoln. He simply didn't display sufficient respect for the Constitution, in my view. By the way, the Constitution **provides** for states' secession; it guarantees

27

that right! The founding fathers foresaw a possible need of such a clause (and rightly so)!

A vote could easily have decided whether people wanted two nations or one. It was autocratic to make that decision from the White House. Lincoln behaved like King Lincoln.

Mason-Dixon Line

That "natural divide" in the US still exists. You see as many confederate flags in the south today as in civil war days, maybe more! Let the south decide NOW if it wants to be "free" of the North. If they do, they should petition the US Congress to permit their secession from the union.

If the south voted against secession, it would probably quell the resentment that has existed for over 100 years. If they voted for secession, Congress would be sorely pressed to refuse it, since they advocate people in *other* countries should be allowed separation rights if they vote that way.

Congress would not again go to war with the South!

Texas is the second most blatant case. Native Texans & many adopted sons of Texas have always felt cheated by the way their state was scooped up into the US. By military force.

The lone star flag has always flown in more places than the US national flag, & evokes considerable emotion and affection.

Here too, a referendum vote for all Texans would soon reveal if they wanted nationhood to replace statehood. I've already conducted a poll of all my Texas subscribers on this separate country issue. I'll reveal it at the end of this chapter.

As an economist I assure you there is no question that any US state, even Rhode Island, could get along economically as a sovereign nation. Texas most certainly could!

There would have been *no* real estate depression in Texas in 1989-90 if Texas had been a country because Washington would not have been the catalyst that caused it, via the self-destructive guarantee of all bank & S&L deposits.

How would the national debt be divided up among states? That would be for a new Continental Congress meeting to resolve, but perhaps the fairest way would be to apportion on the basis of population per nation. If the South (Dixie) had 25% of the population, it would get 25% of the debt. But also, 25% of the gold in Fort Knox. And 25% of the foreign currencies in the NY Federal Reserve.

The US has become ungovernable, financially. Its debt burden is crushing & there is no solution so long as Congress is structured as it is, with unlimited terms of office, pork-barrel tactics, & off-budget fiddling.

Chopping up the country may be the only way to solve the financial problem, not so much because the chop creates money (though it will stimulate growth wonderfully & create lots of new industries & jobs) but because the present "system" in Washington isn't working!!! Exclamation point times 3. You can't dissolve the USA, but you can break it up & thus change the system, so that problems CAN be solved. The present political infrastructure absolutely *precludes* a solution. I suspect most hard money advocates will agree with me.

Even many fiat-money followers are disgusted with the status quo.

It's axiomatic that most or perhaps every new country or political framework reaches a bureaucratic crunch point after a certain number of years. A critical mass. Boondoggling builds & builds; govt. becomes incestuous, multiplies beyond the ability of the population to afford it. A house-cleaning is then necessary to change the system. That has happened repeatedly in Europe & Asia. The US is well overdue for a spring clean.

Reducing the terms of Congress would go a long way to revive the US. But that is unlikely to happen since Congress itself would have to vote itself virtually out of office. And even if by some miracle it did, it isn't a complete financial remedy as is dividing the US into several parts.

I would then urge those parts to limit the terms of their legislators from day one so the old scenario doesn't repeat.

What about the rest of the US? Well, there's *California*, isn't there? A state with a bigger GNP than over half the world's nations. The question is not whether California should be a nation, but whether it would prefer to be two nations, north & south. I'm neutral but lean toward two. But let locals decide that on the same ballot as their decision to withdraw from Washington.

The ballot would ask: Do you want California to withdraw from the USA & become a separate country, yes or no? And: if California becomes separate would you favor two nations, i.e., North California and South California?

Other divisions? The rest of the west, the *mountain states*, may or may not wish to be separate. They're big enough, bigger than all of Europe. They're *entitled* to vote on it.

The *middle west*—the Great Lake states? Perhaps. They have a mentality all their own. Maybe they want a government all their own.

New England a nation too? There is hardly any doubt the New England culture & history & outlook is special. Maybe they are anxious to be separate if there is an opportunity provided through other areas doing so.

There may be those who conceive of different structuring. I would hope readers will write me with ideas on this & other aspects, which we can incorporate into the sequel to this volume.

Writer Robie Cafayan has suggested to me: "Why not 50 states equal *50 countries*?" There is no structural reason against it. Think of the opportunities *that* would throw up for new jobs!!

For example, maybe Florida wants to be the *Republic of Florida*, a land of its own, where dreams are fulfilled. And maybe New York State wants to be *New York, the nation*. New Yorkers have always felt they were a special breed. And so they are.

But I won't speculate further on these ideas.

Using the rough suggestions above, & ignoring the possibility of Florida & New York for the moment, or 50 nations, the US would then be transformed into: Dixie, Texas, South California, North California, Mountain states, Middle west, New England, i.e., 7 in all (but it could easily be 9 or 15). Not all 7 regions may want independence. That's OK too. There can be 3 or 4 or 5 divisions instead of 7; it doesn't matter. Go with the flow. That's what has NOT happened in the past. Some people (e.g., Abe Lincoln) forced a square peg into a round hole. He said "It ought to fit!" We live with the awkward results of his force.

The actual NAMES for these new nations I will cheerfully leave to locals to have fun with formulating. Contests could be held by the local newspapers & I hope newspapers will open their columns to discuss the entire matter. Hometown newspapers are the lifeblood of the US & they deserve a key role in formulating the debate. I'm probably prejudiced, having owned 13 small-town newspapers in my younger days.

Local radio & TV. A natural for a talk show.

If you let your imagination run loose, you can visualize all manner of new businesses & activity that will crop up when/if the US becomes 7 or 9 nations. E.g., flags, stamps, coins, currency, passports, private companies to run the highways, insurance companies to run private social security systems for 7-9 new nations, swarms of new diplomats for the UN & UN agencies & IMF & GATT, etc., defense structures, National Guards transferring into regular army, private schools to take over from govt. schools, map makers, publications devoted to the new nations, new coast guard svc., new Congressmen & Senators, etc. A complete list could fill two pages.

It's not unthinkable that the stimulation caused by this division of nations would be enough to *pull the world out* of its recession, cum-depression, especially when/if you presume that the new nations *could* be functioning as privatized govt. & with Adam Smith philosophy, anti-Keynesian, low-tax (maximum 10%) entities. That's **not** a given but it's a possibility that is offered by starting a new structure. (I suspect political jobs in the new nations would attract many high-caliber women & men who now don't wish to live in Washington, or other present world capital cities, nor move their children away from home to do so.)

For example, if you cut China into 8 parts, surely some/most of them would seize on the opportunity to follow more closely the

Hong Kong type of economy & politics than the communist doctrine. If so, the power generated by that economic freedom would be a nuclear-size explosion of business, trade, enterprise.

I realize I'm making a credibility leap in assuming this is possible in China. But, if China sees that 10 other countries are holding referendums on this & some are putting it into practice, it may in time penetrate the Chinese mentality, especially as the aged old guard is replaced with a younger generation. As my dear old now-departed friend, economic philosopher Antony Fisher used to say: *"Ideas have consequences."* And it was the Chinese who invented the concept of a drop of water eventually wearing away even the hardest, biggest rock.

The same can be applied to the separate states in the USA. Give Nevada its independence and it would grow at four times its present rate, in my opinion. We'll have to deal with the nuts & bolts of some of this in the sequel to this volume. There won't be room nor time to include every aspect here. It is easy to envision an annual sequel.

Gold Backing

If I were asked to be the finance minister for South California, for example (and I hope I'm not!!!), I would not want the USA dollar circulating in my nation because it has *no backing* & too much debt. Some would propose the US $Dollar continue to circulate for 5 years, or some such interim period. I would either refuse such a compromise or limit it to a very brief period, e.g., 6 mos., while we printed our own money (California Dollars, or "California nuggets"), bought gold for backing the currency & created the hardest currency on the planet. We would put an end to Keynesian deficit financing. No, it wouldn't be very easy. It would be very difficult, but it is possible, given the right structure. It's like Judo. A small man can move a big man, using leverage. The impossible becomes possible when you use correct engineering principles—of finance, psychology & incentive. It would be easier than critics will think.

You can see, by starting afresh you have a chance to set up systems with all the accumulated knowledge of the past & present day, without being burdened with rules & laws passed in haste long ago which are difficult to get changed.

I would propose that every new nation's legislature, upon being elected to service the new nation, start with *zero laws* on the books, & have to **review** *every* prior law—& either drop it, change it or accept it for the new nation. We'll breed a new generation of Founding Fathers!!

Laws seem only to grow, never shrink. They don't remove old laws. They only add new ones. So, here would be a platinum & golden opportunity to start afresh. In time, the new nation too will be encrusted with barnacles, but for 50-100 years things would run wonderfully well, free of past cobwebs & many wrong theories.

And just as the US was an improvement on Europe because it was a fresh start without outmoded laws to inhibit its growth, so the new reconstituted nations will be an improvement on the *old* USA.

This is a "gift from heaven" kind of opportunity that I hope will be seen by citizens & talked up in the media & then implemented via the ballot box. An historic opportunity for people to vote themselves new nations with the snap of a finger, creating a magical new world.

If this occurs in sync with certain other nations doing the same, the multiplier effect will be magnificent.

We could solve MOST of man's problems if we handle this right. Even if there is some bungling along the line, the new structure will still bring overwhelmingly positive results, in my opinion.

If you agree, I hope you will ask your local newspaper to review this book, & ask local radio & TV stations & press for interviews & talk shows with myself or my research director Gordon Frisch. We will divide up the world between us. I'll take Europe, Australia, South Africa, & the Far East. He'll take North & South America, North & Central Africa & the Mid-East. We may need more help! Gordon has worked with me on my newsletter for 3 years & we think much alike. He can carry the case to more microphones than I can alone. Maybe I can get Anton Keller, another able research

editor for this book, friend, & freedom fighter, to speak in the
Germanic & French-speaking cities. If we're invited.

But don't depend on us. Tackle it yourself. Talk it up in your
men's & women's clubs. Start clubs for the movement. Think of the
fun it will be. *The South Shall Rise Again Club.* Sign: *We're not
just whistling Dixie.* Or **Middle West Inc.** Or *Florida a Republic.* Or
North California Can Stand Alone Club. Or *Mountain States Land.*
Or how about: **Great New England.**

In 6-9 months, you will probably have written me enough new
ideas to fill many of the pages of the sequel to this book.

Two heads are better than one. 20,000 heads are even better.
Write me either at the International Commission for the De-
centralization of the World's Nations (ICDWN), P.O. Box 2376,
Silver Spring, MD 20915, USA, or P.O. Box 7337, CH-8023, Zurich,
Switzerland. I don't know if I can answer every letter, but I'll
certainly read every one, and action all the good ideas.

Maybe some of you would like to be coordinators for action
in your area & would like having your name & address available
to others in your area. I guess we could act as a channel through
which people get together for that purpose.

Texas

Before closing this chapter, here are the results I promised you
of the Texas poll I conducted in April/May, 1991. I sent the following
form letter to all the Texas subscribers of HSL (the International Harry
Schultz Letter):

> Dear Texan hslm:
> I am writing an electrifying new (political) book. I think
> it will be an earth-shaker. I need your help. Would you
> please answer the following question, below, & mail it
> to me in Monte Carlo immediately? You don't need to
> sign your name.
>
> Question: Would you like to see Texas become a
> separate country?

Tick one: ☐ Yes   ☐ No
            ☐ Lean toward Yes ☐ Lean toward No
If you wish to add a comment, please do. Thank you.

Harry D. Schultz
A reply envelope is enclosed for your convenience.

The results? **60%** voted yes. **13%** voted no. **24%** leaned toward yes. **2%** leaned toward no. 2% no opinion. (Figures rounded off) If you add the yes & lean-yes together, they total a staggering **84% positive**, to a combined no & lean-no vote of **15% negative**.

Among the comments were these: A great idea...Texas is a *state of mind*. Many of us would welcome the opportunity to be a separate country *again*...Texas has enough problems without becoming a country...The sooner the better! How can I help?...Yes, if it could be set up with a more functional political & legal system. Our present country is headed toward self-destruct, due to the rapid decay of our political system & legal systems...Yes, we could then have the USA send billions to us...Would vote for it...It would eliminate the Feds, but make many other states jealous...Ultimately everything perishes & failure triumphs through the venality & unworthiness of the crowd (Editors note: I agree & that's why it's necessary to start over again, every 100 yrs. or so. It took over 100 to virtually destroy the US Constitution; it was *inevitable*, for the reasons you correctly state)...

Yes, in order to send a message to our politicians...Yes, due mostly to my displeasure with the US Congress than traditional Texas separatism...Yes, but my only concern would be regarding military protection against a dictator getting hold of Mexico. (Editor's note: every new US sub-nation would make treaties with the others for joint military protection)...Yes, let's do it!...No, I fear the hispanics gaining control. (Editor's note: I don't think that will be affected either way; in fact you would have a better chance for harmony if everything were handled locally). Yes, this may be the best way to have our OWN country (along HSL lines)...We're being strangled by our govt.; we need conservative ideas, less govt., less tax, no socialism, promote self-help, independence of govt. & individual. We need TOTAL freedom...Yes, with no IRS or state income tax & a different head of state. (Editor's note: a stiff sales tax could replace all other taxes & be a more fair system)....Yes, but I have concerns the Texas politicos may be as bad as Washington idiots. (Editor's note: It's easier to watch locally based politicians than those who are far out of state)...Yes, it would be a tremendous challenge, something to work toward, a utopia. (Editor's note: exactly; new structures foster new idealism, hope, energy. Never mind if the energy runs out in 100 years; they can jump-start again then.)

One reader wrote: "I wish Texas had never joined the union. The federal govt. is destroying our lives by making almost everything illegal. It's time to plan to leave for wherever civil liberties still abound. Most Texans want to secede now. Bumper stickers all over say: 'Secede from the Union'."

Another wrote: "As a republic, a separate nation, Texas could be partitioned into 5 separate states with Austin as capital. The US turned its back on Texas in 1985-87—the southwest depression. Texas has ample resources (people & natural) to survive & prosper. Remember the Alamo!"

In sum, the majority want to TRY it! They are cynical & not blind to the problems but they feel there is more to gain than lose, & I think these Texans are right.

For our sequel book, we'll conduct polls (if Gallup doesn't beat us to it) of many other states. In my opinion, we will get a similar result because people are fed up with the present situation & see no HOPE with the current system. Only by (peacefully) changing the system, can solutions evolve, in my view.

If nothing is done, the USA is headed for the status of a cheap labor, banana republic, which services other nation's needs. The standard of living will continue to fall & increase its rate of decline.

Chapter 6

The Kurds

Iraq deserves **remaking**. Some supporters of the "New World Order" think otherwise. They want to keep Iraq intact, so there is a balance of power in the middle east. Obviously that has merit.

But politicians sometimes (mostly?) get their priorities wrong.

The first and primary need is to assure the Kurds a **permanently safe** bastion. To give them an *autonomous* zone within Iraq is the method being negotiated over as this is written. But most Kurd leaders in the field don't believe such an agreement would hold up. I agree.

The dictator of no morality, Saddam Hussein, has previously made the same deal, on almost identical terms, with most of the same Kurd leaders. Saddam went back on the deal when his military power was sufficient. He *will* again. That is as predictable as any personality trait can be. As predictable as Ronald Reagan's warm and charming smile. Reagan can't stop being a loveable person and Saddam can't stop being a snake. Maggie Thatcher can't stop being the way she is, firm, resolute and high-minded.

So, since a deal with Saddam is unthinkable, except for day dreamers, the alternatives are: a permanent UN peace-keeping force in the north of Iraq, which is hardly a long-term solution, or, giving the Kurds their own nation.

The latter is obviously the best choice.

And that must be done very soon before current flexibilities become rigidities.

The need goes beyond that, though it is unlikely we can cure the total need immediately. The overall requirement is for restoration of the Kurdish nation, cut partly out of Iran & USSR & Turkey & Iraq & Syria. This requires these other nations giving up some soil.

But our view is that the soil doesn't *belong* to the political leaders; it belongs to the people who live there, and if they prefer flag A over flag B, then let them have it. You can't win fighting that fact.

Kurdistan is a real nation, but you don't find it on a political map, only on tribal/cultural/ancient maps, and of course in millions of hearts.

When the present borders were drawn, which cancelled out Kurdistan and gave a piece each to USSR, Turkey, Iran, Iraq, Syria, the planners were foolish.

No need however to keep that wrong deed ongoing.

You don't need a referendum for this issue, nor will any of the countries involved ever give their people a chance to vote on such matters. But a Middle East conference to discuss various subjects could readily put this one on the table.

If they don't, or if they do and nothing much happens, the Kurd problem won't go away.

"Giving" the Kurds a nation within Iraq is the first, most urgent step. I don't like the word "giving" because it doesn't belong to Saddam or Iraq. It belongs to the Kurds and always has.

Freeing up the rest of Kurdistan will then become, via precedent, an easier matter to negotiate.

This blueprint is fairly simple, as all great truths/formulas are. They are usually so apparent they go unnoticed. The best place to hide a truth is in plain sight.

Joseph de Courcy's excellent *Intelligence Digest* (17 Rodney Rd., Cheltenham, UK) tells us "The Kurds number *30 million* throughout the 5 nations (mentioned above), the fourth most numerous people in the Middle East. They remain one of the largest races to be denied an independent state.

"Like all the other subjects of the Ottoman empire, the Kurds were to have achieved statehood under the 1920 Treaty of Sevres signed by the allies after the collapse of Turkey and the break-up of its empire. But the treaty was never ratified, and 3 years later, the Treaty of Lausanne made no mention of an independent Kurdistan.

"Despite the attempts of all the 5 nations involved, it has proved impossible to extinguish the Kurdish desire for an independent state." DeCourcy agrees that now is the time for the Kurds to seize a chance for a Kurd state in northern Iraq.

By the way, the last recognized Kurdish state was Mahabad, in Iran, which was dissolved by Iran in 1947.

The London Sunday Times reports (May 5, 1991) the Kurds had full regional sovereignty in the Middle Ages.

Douglas Hurd, UK foreign secretary, is to be praised for insisting the Kurds be saved from the Iraq massacre, and then protected. He led the West in this initiative. Where he went off was in declaring that an autonomous region within Iraq would suffice. I presume he was forced to say that by the US State Dept. who are off on another of their infamous & classic foreign policy errors.

Turning to the Shiites: some say that full independence for Kurds means a nation state for the Shiites. I don't follow that logic. There is no history to support that claim. There are no RULES for who gets and who doesn't get. The nearest we have to rules are precedent, history, the record. Here the Kurds win hands down. Whether the Shiites deserve or need a separate state is something for diplomats to examine, but it is not a given that it is an *automatic* trade-off with the Kurds. If anything, it may be a pink herring.

It is said (via Ash Shaab, Cairo) the US State Dept. doesn't want an Islam Fundamentalist take-over of Baghdad, especially Shiites, because they would link-up with Iran, creating a big (anti-West) war machine. In that case, giving the Shiites a *very small* enclave nation-state in the Iraq south, *on* the Saudi border, not touching Iran, would isolate them from Baghdad, making a take-over of Iraq by Shiites less likely.

In any case, trade-off or not, the Kurds *must* be given their own dirt. Not autonomy. A flag.

Chapter 7

Canada & Australia

These lovely countries are taken together here since they are twins in many ways. They are both ex-British Empire. Both are commonwealth nations. They have similar size populations and vast, largely unsettled, land. Both their stock markets & economies move, oddly, in approximate harmony. Both are mineral-oriented. Both have vocal farmers. Both are English-speaking. Both have trouble throwing up quality leaders, with rare exceptions. Both populations harbor considerable resentment against their capital cities, who are considered to be remote from the people at large, both physically and mentally.

Now to take them separately:

Canada

Canada is already a prime candidate for new borders, with Quebec on the very edge of a divorce from the rest of Canada. It is a matter for daily debate in Canada. I have championed the cause of Quebec separatism in my newsletter for 15 years or so. I did so because there is tremendous resentment by the English over being saddled with a stupid bi-lingual law shoved through parliament by left-wing ex-premier Pierre Trudeau. French is NOT the natural language of most of Canada, so it is ridiculous for them to have every tube of toothpaste printed in 2 languages, plus a million other such items.

Nor were the French Canadian residents of Quebec kindly disposed toward English speaking residents in their province. They

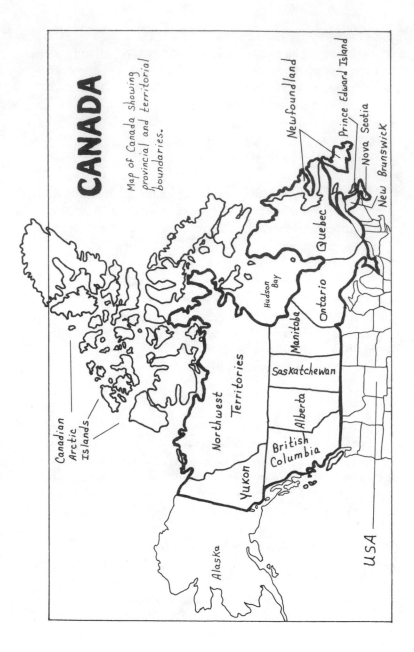

CANADA

Map of Canada showing provincial and territorial boundaries.

Newfoundland

Prince Edward Island

Nova Scotia

New Brunswick

Quebec

Hudson Bay

Ontario

Manitoba

Saskatchewan

Northwest Territories

Alberta

British Columbia

Canadian Arctic Islands

Yukon

Alaska

USA

forbad English signs over stores! It has been a one-sided relationship for decades. Quebec got special treatment that other provinces didn't get, and demanded more of the same. All the understandable resentment can be changed into friendliness by a divorce. Let Quebec go its own way. It will change frowns into smiles. Then the English speakers can visit Quebec as a "quaint" foreign country, & vice versa. There are horses for courses, as Canadian friend Paul Penna says.

But this is only half of the Canadian story. Other parts of Canada are not pleased with Ottawa as their destiny director. The Atlantic provinces might be better off as a separate nation. So, too, the prairie provinces.

BC (British Columbia) is already a separate thought-process place. It is full of speculators, including the Chinese imports who are speculating on their future here vs. Hong Kong.

Ontario can easily go it alone. At a minimum, Canada could make at least 5 nations, if not more. The Northern territory could make a sixth, far larger than any European nation.

Canada already lives in two worlds, has two (or more) mind sets. It is too big for a single country, just as is the USA and the USSR, both of which should never have become their present size, in my opinion.

I've lived in Canada at length, crossed it from Atlantic to Pacific, slowly by car and also by train, and stayed in every province, and did a speaking tour from coast to coast. But despite that exposure, I don't claim to know it well enough to propose specific divisions, except in the general terms above. But I do claim to know there is genuine discontent with Ottawa making decisions for Edmonton and Saint Johns Island and Toronto and Vancouver. Globe & Mail columnist Jeffrey Simpson speaks of the possibility of splitting Ontario in two as it is too big and powerful. I'll cheerfully leave such decisions to Canucks. I am content to have pointed in the general direction of invigoration via reallocation of nationhoods.

Australia

Now to Australia: it's too big to be one country. Perth, which I love, is nothing like Sydney, which I also like but for different reasons. Nor is Adelaide like Cairns. Melbourne is like no other place on earth. The artificial capital of Canberra is an *abomination*, very much like Washington, DC in mini-size. Each of the present states of Australia could easily be a country, including Tasmania. Each state could, in fact, make two nations, but perhaps that is too imaginative and ambitious, so we'll have to settle for one each, I suspect.

The political system is so twisted (not in theory, but in practice) that a break-up and start-over with different units may be just what the flying doctor ordered for this lovely land—that never *quite* succeeds. It's always on the verge, rather like Brazil. It SHOULD click, but somehow never does.

I know Australia intimately, every state, every city, and almost every wine. I've crossed it many times, done lecture tours coast to coast, appeared on all the TV and in all the press. I'm extremely fond of Australia, and because I wish it the very best, I recommend most wholeheartedly that Ozzies do a chop-chop and separate themselves into separate nations, instead of the current separate states.

Chapter 8

The USSR—Quo Vadis?

An editorial in the Financial Times of London Dec. 21, 1990 (headlined: The end of perestroika) said in two sentences what we surely all know but few put forth so neatly as a premise: "The Soviet Union is too large and too unwieldy. Moscow always held too much power."

But then I part company with the FT. They say the solution is in the creation of a looser federal system. While that might help a bit, it is NOT a solution, merely a palliative, a bone thrown to the dog to keep him from biting you. Federalization would sanctify the former military takeovers of the captive nations. Moscow will never give up any powers that matter, to a federation. Only permission for locals to clean their own streets without directives from the Kremlin.

The USSR is history's worst example of a nation put together by a committee, as is often spoken of a camel. Former free nations were taken over by the Soviet war machine and it is time to set them free.

I prefer the thinking of ex-Congressman Ron Paul who says in his Political Report newsletter: "The three Baltic nations ought to be independent of Moscow. So, too, the Ukraine, Byelorussia, Georgia, Armenia, all the captive nations of the USSR have the right to be free."

He then quotes the great Austrian economist Ludwig von Mises who said, over 70 years ago: "No people and no part of a people shall be held against its will in a political association it does not want."

The 15 Soviet republics should, in equity, be divided into perhaps 20 nations. The *Russian* and *Kazakhstan* republics are far too large to be only one, cover too many different ethnic groups to be compatible.

Recent bloody fighting in south USSR reveals the desperate need for self-determination. Soviet troops have intervened viciously to no beneficial end. The *Armenian-Azerbaijan* area needs a ballot vote and a neutral body to advise on a fair racial balance break-up into sectors in which each can live at peace.

Georgia already behaves as though it were an independent nation.

The *Ukraine* has been a submerged nation for decades, is now reclaiming its place on the map of the continent. It is 52 million strong. It has begun charting its own independent foreign policy. It was an independent nation in modern history from 1917 to 1920 and was then conquered by Russia's Bolsheviks and granted sovereignty only on paper.

In 1945 Stalin found it expedient to demand that the *Ukraine* and *Byelorussia* be given founding member status along with the USSR in the United Nations. Stalin thought it not only placated these states but gave him three votes at the UN. That dirty trick is now backfiring, as justice finally wins.

In Sept. 1990, Hungary recognized the Ukraine as a sovereign state. In Oct., Polish officials visited the capital Kiev and signed a Ukrainian-Polish declaration of friendship. On Nov. 19 a treaty between Ukraine & the Russian federation was signed, an historic breakthrough. That treaty by-passed the Kremlin. The Ukraine asked the French to allow Ukraine observer status at the CSCE summit. Shevardnadze denounced the call.

But the Ukrainians pressed their case. Speaking at a Paris press conference, Messrs. Drach and Dmytro Pavlychko put the world into the Big Picture thus: "Europe cannot *end* at the borders of the USSR. Sooner or later the Helsinki process with its emphasis on promoting democratic values & international understanding will have to take account of the spectacular collapse of the Stalinists-

Brezhnevist system not only in Eastern and Central Europe but also in the Soviet Union. Democratic Europe has moral & political responsibility to support the states struggling to extricate themselves from the collapsing Soviet empire."

These are brave and inspiring words. The West must follow-up with its most potent weapon: *recognition* of various republics, like the Ukraine, as independent sovereign states. Germany recently opened a consulate in Kiev, and Canada will soon do so. The question of a US consulate in Kiev is apparently under consideration. (I recommend the book *Soviet Disunion: A History of the Nationalities Problem in the USSR* (Macmillan 1990). Bohdan Nhaylo is co-author.)

I found a NY Times column by William Safire of May 10, 1991, inspiring. He encourages the US to use credit guarantees for investment in the Baltic nations, and a Baltic development bank. Richard Nixon, a recent Soviet visitor, agrees. Says US should be helping reformers in all of the republics, instead of pressing credits into the dead hand of the Gorbocracy.

Safire urges the US to warn the Kremlin that any economic punishment of the Baltics would trigger US counter-coercion. Says US should also lean on Soviets to accept the Balts as observers at the next meeting of Security & Cooperation in Europe. At Helsinki-II, March 1992, the US should link its attendance to the full participation of the Balts as Euro nations. Safire delights us by saying the Nobel committee should make up for its abysmal judgment of the recent past by awarding the next Peace Prize to Vytautas Landsbergis, Lithuania's president & symbol of Baltic independence. Safire concludes with these wonderful words: "Keep the heat on; free the Baltics, *change the world*."

Changing the world is approximately the title & the aim of this book and I'm excited to have William Safire stating his view that we can *do* it via such methodry. I most certainly agree. If enough of us feel this way, we *CAN* change the world.

The next few pages are written by Anton Keller, one of our research team. His approach is more diplomatic and *traditionally* political than mine. Also more academic. Non-academics will find it slow going. Academics will probably love it. (Anton also publishes Selex magazine in Europe.)

From Roots to Rots to Rights

In 1914, the Russian Empire, after having sold Alaska to the United States in 1867, embraced most of the continent—from Finland, the Baltic States, Poland (with no direct access to the sea) and Moldavia to Wladivostok and beyond (excepting, e.g., the Kurile islands). It had commerce agreements a.o. with France, Great Britain and the U.S., providing for *most-favored-nation treatment in most commercial areas.* Neither Lenin nor any of his successors abrogated these treaties which, though dormant, can be reanimated.

Expanded trade and commerce is crucial for the herculian clean-up of the economic mess due to 70 years of mismanagement of human and natural resources.

Either as separate remnants of a split-up USSR, or as a newly constituted confederation, they might benefit from these forgotten bilateral treaties even with members of the EC (whose basic Rome Treaty, in art.234, specifies that foregoing treaties take *precedence* over EC laws). This may significantly contribute to the *viability* of those republics opting for *genuine independence,* particularly if their leaders will never lose sight of such principles as: *Reforms can be considered successful if (as a result):*

- *citizens will be less inclined to emigrate.*
- *foreign professionals will be more willing to come, reside and work in the land, and*
- *foreign capital will be more attracted to come and stay in the country.*

After the Referendum of March 17, 1991

The Referendum intended to take the Soviet people's pulse on the future of their centralized union, broken up into fragments. Of the USSR's 15 republics, only *five* strictly followed directives from Moscow, asking their voters bewilderingly this *loaded* question:

Do you consider it necessary to preserve the union of Soviet Socialist Republics as a renewed federation of equal sovereign republics, in which human rights and the freedoms of all nationalities will be fully guaranteed?

Their score of yes votes is: *Byelorussia* (a full UN Member)— 83%; *Azerbaijan*—93%; *Kirgizia*—95%; *Tajikistan*—96%; *Turkmenia*—98%. These figures, The Economist of March 23 observed wryly, are "suspiciously approaching the good old days of 99.9% Communist voting." 94% of the Kazakhstan voters said yes to the chopped-down question: "Do you consider it necessary to preserve the USSR as a union of sovereign states?" Russia, Ukraine and Uzbekistan—accounting for some 79% of the USSR's population—added their own future-indicative questions. Almost as many of the potential 100 million *Russian* voters (70%) said yes to Boris Yeltsin's question, "Do you want direct elections to Russia's presidency?" as to Mr. Gorbachev's (71%). The Moscovites, to 85%, wanted direct election of its mayor. And the imported Kurile Islanders, to 88%, did not want to become part of Japan. The *Ukraine* (another full-fledged "independent" UN member State) asked:

Do you want the Ukraine to be part of a Union of Soviet Sovereign States on the basis of its declaration of sovereignty?

80% said yes, versus 74% to Mr. Gorbachev's questions. (*Uzbekistan* did the same with similar results.) The West Ukraine also asked: "Do you want the Ukraine to be an independent state?" Nearly 90% said yes. *Six republics—Lithuania, Estonia, Latvia, Georgia, Armenia and Moldavia—boycotted the vote and did not sign the new Union Treaty, as the nine others did on April 23, 1991.* On Feb. 9, 1991, over 90% of 75% of the eligible *Lithuanians* voted for independence (thus even meeting the Soviet secession law's requirement of two-thirds of all eligible voters). The *Georgian* and the *Baltic* governments already refuse to recognize Soviet law. On March 3, 1990, 73% of *Latvians* and 77% of *Estonians* voted also for independence, with about half of the Russians living there estimated to have boycotted that poll.

Georgia held its own independence poll on March 31, 1991. *Armenia* will hold its poll on September 21, 1991; it refused to participate in the March 17, 1991 referendum also for fear it might thus undermine its interests concerning the embattled enclave Nagorno-Karabakh.

The UN's encouraging and confusing outlook for the USSR's short- and medium-term future puts a spotlight on Soviet leaders' actions/inactions. And it makes mere shadows of possible deviations from what the West expects them to risk.

A variation of this bleak outlook—say a Soviet GNP decline of only 10% and less inflation—could be expected, in the view of the Washington correspondent of NZZ. Provided the agreement of April 23, 1991, for a mutually beneficial structure of *genuinely separate sovereign* republics freely joining resources in a *real* Confederation, turned out to be an *acceptable* basis for overdue (and inevitable) fundamental reforms deserving the name. Also, according to Professor Vladimir Treml (Duke University), the USSR's underground economy accounts for 21-25% of its GNP. With the presence of market-relevant structures, individual capabilities and administration (or forced tolerances), such a strong and de-criminalizable underground market, in the eyes of Professor Treml, makes a *total collapse of the Soviet economy not inevitable.*

On the other hand, and what all this really means with regard to the results above of the USSR's March 17 Referendum, it's fair to say the USSR's state of the Union is unstable and apparently out of control. This deteriorating background makes it unreasonable and even frivolous to interpret the results as a public mandate for more of the same. Rather, they seem to have a ring of a *general public outcry in favor of fundamental reforms.*

Paths to Implement the People's Will

The best case for devolution is that *policies should be forged at the most practical local level.* This message seems increasingly to be understood by both the people and the leaders who are participating in USSR's reform debate. Attention should be focused on ways and means to help these processes. One potent vehicle for helping along the educational/structural/economic reforms may—paradoxically—be found in the military, which is used to discipline and execute orders, and often has the best if not the only usable infrastructure and competence left to rebuild a downtrodden society (see the ground-breaking "IRON MOUNTAIN REPORT—On the Desirability and Feasibility of Peace," Levin, edit. New York, 1968).

Another politically potent instrument may be found in *external political self-interest*—as demonstrated when, in June 1989,

West German Chancellor Helmut Kohl, and the Soviet leader Mikhail Gorbachev, reached an agreement to use [the Kaliningrad Oblast of the Russian Soviet Federated Socialist Republic, the former German East Prussia, situated between Lithuania and Poland on the Baltic Sea] as the location for a *German-populated* constituent *republic* of the USSR. For Bonn, this solution is seen as a means of stemming the flood of German emigres from the Soviet Union. For Moscow, it is seen as a solution to an ethnic problem that has been dogging the USSR for years. (WSJ 10/20/90).

Chapter 9

It's High Noon in Africa

E thnic hostility is the engine powering most of the wars in today's world and nowhere is this better exemplified than in the conflict-ridden African continent. And nowhere would redrawing and creation of *new borders* to coincide with *natural and ethnic* divisions so drastically reduce irredentist claims, conflict and suffering. *Pre*-colonial Africa was a complex amalgam of thousands of tribes, languages and fiefdoms which existed in a perpetual *state of balance* based on geographical and ethnic boundaries. European colonialists then rampaged through Africa for decades, built giant land empires and forcefully united totally disparate ethnic groups. Upon departure, the Colonial empires left a cartographic disaster guaranteed to create conflict.

One of the most obvious natural boundaries on Earth is the Sahel, the east-west region across central Africa marking the transition from the world's largest desert to bush and jungle (see map). This natural boundary is easily seen by the naked eye from space and it appears as the major feature on virtually every topographical map of Africa ever drawn. To the south of the Sahel lies Black tribal Africa, primarily a region of lush jungle, grasslands and fantastic mineral wealth. North of the Sahel lies the barren Sahara Desert, nomads, primarily Moslem peoples and some oil. For all practical purposes, the Sahel splits the continent of Africa into two major sub-continents. Each sub-continent naturally breaks down into many smaller regions on the basis of geography and ethnicity.

When the colonial powers departed Africa, they left countries

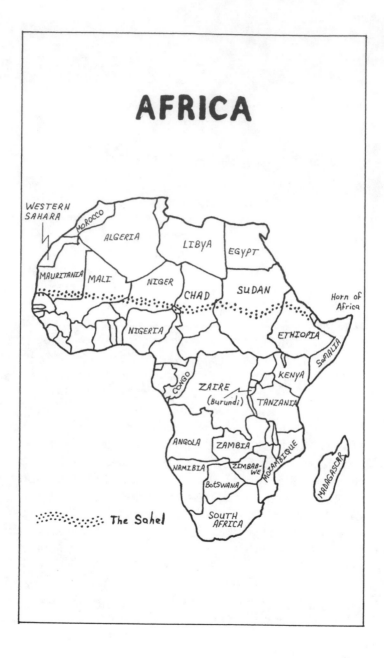

with disputable boundaries straddling the Sahel, forcefully uniting parts of dissimilar sub-continents. Predictable and devastating conflicts ensued and persist to this day, particularly in the Sahelian countries of Ethiopia, Sudan and Chad. Conflict exists to a lesser degree in Niger, Mali and Mauritania, because their borders somewhat coincided with the Sahelian boundary to begin with. A close look at some of the ravaged countries of the Sahel reveals obvious problems and obvious solutions.

Ethiopia

To understand present day Ethiopia, known as Abyssinia until the 1950s, a brief historical and geographical summary is necessary. Ethiopia's central highlands, which include the capital of Addis Ababa, consists of mountainous plateaus and inaccessible valleys. This area is populated by the Amhara tribe who were converted to Christianity in the 4th century. In the 7th century, Islam had spread to surrounding regions and the Christian Amhara were essentially cut off and isolated until European explorers rediscovered them in the 19th century. Throughout the Middle Ages they warred with neighboring Moslem tribes and Ethiopia's size expanded and contracted with victories and defeats.

While the European colonists (Italians, French and British) were establishing themselves along the coast of the Horn of Africa in the late 1800s, Emperor Menelik II doubled Ethiopia's size by conquering southwest Ethiopia's Oromo Region and southeastern Ethiopia's Ogaden Region. The Ogaden is peopled by nomadic Moslem Somalis, ethnic blood brothers to the people of neighboring Somalia.

Emperor Haile Selassie, who claimed descent from King Solomon and the Queen of Sheba, came to power in 1916 and ruled until 1974 when a Marxist regime took over and civil war broke out. In 1962, pursuant to a UN territorial mandate, Haile Selassie annexed the Red Sea region of Eritrea, and, for the first time in history, Ethiopia had an outlet to the sea. Not surprisingly, Eritrea, neighboring Tigray and the Ogaden and Oromo Regions refused to be ruled from the capital in Addis Ababa and in the mid 1970s, civil war broke out as the senile Haile Selassie fell from power. The new Marxist regime was able to contain the civil war and the integrity of Ethiopia's borders only with massive military & economic aid from Cuba and the Soviet Union.

Rebellion continues today; however the decline of the Soviet Empire and its inability to sustain far-flung client states has played into the hands of the conquered. Addis Ababa fell to Eritrean and Tigrean rebel forces in late May 1991 as Ethiopia's brutal leader Mengistu fled the country.

The next likely leaders of Ethiopia—the Tigreans—are also Marxist, so Ethiopia's future isn't particularly bright. The Eritreans, also Marxist, plan to form their own nation in their traditional homeland on the Red Sea. However, there's hope that lack of a Soviet wet nurse will cause both the Eritreans and Tigreans to consider abandoning their failed Marxist ideology in favor of a better system. Ethiopia could begin liberating itself from Marxist oppression, poverty and future conflict by granting autonomy to regions with historical ethnic identities.

We suggest granting independence or complete autonomy to the ethnically distinct regions of Oromo, Ogaden, Eritrea and the mountainous central highlands of Ethiopia (including Tigray, since it's always been closely linked with the Amhara in Ethiopia's central highlands and isn't seeking complete autonomy). Strength and peace lie in disunity. In Ethiopia, a country as big as France, Spain and Portugal combined, *bigger* has *never* been *better,* and *smaller* would be *stronger* and more *peaceful.*

Sudan

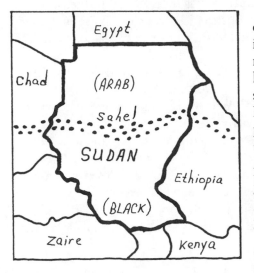

Sudan is a classic example of colonial imperialism and map-making folly. It is Africa's largest country, half the size of the US or western Europe. Two-thirds of the population lies north of the Sahel and its Moslem Arabic inhabitants look to Egypt and bow to Mecca. The other one-third inhabits the south in a Texas-size chunk of Black equatorial Africa, having pagan and Christian roots in Central and East Africa. By virtue of intense colonial competition between France and Britain in the 1800s, Sudan was forcefully united under one flag although neither nation had any use whatsoever for the endless expanses of desert and swamp. Although Egypt conquered Sudan in 1819, Britain conquered Egypt in the 1870s and so ruled by proxy until independence in 1956.

Under the British, northern Sudan was ruled in Arabic from Khartoum while southern Sudan was ruled in English from Juba. Although colonial Britain administered Sudan as though it were two separate countries and obviously recognized the practicality of fixing a boundary between them, they left without doing so. A simple established line drawn in the edge of the sand could have prevented untold suffering for generations to come.

Since Sudan's independence in 1956, there's been continuous conflict or outright civil war between the powerful ruling Arabs in Khartoum and the persecuted Blacks in the south. Millions of Blacks have been killed in genocidal fashion or died during drought years as Khartoum purposely choked off mega-tonnages of plentiful international food aid. The situation has deteriorated further in recent years with the imposition of strict Islamic law, the rise of Moslem fundamentalism and the establishment of cozy relations with radical Libya. John Garang, a US-educated Christian from the Dinka tribe, has arisen as a leader trying to unify the tribes of southern Sudan against the Khartoum government. But he's hopelessly outgunned and can't match the Arab world's military and materiel assistance to the Khartoum regime.

There's a screaming need for a new international east-west boundary running along the Sahel through the middle of Sudan (see map). Giant strife-stricken Sudan needs to become two separate nations to recognize and honor the irreconcilable differences between north and south. Unremitting pain, suffering and poverty will prevail until a recognized international boundary separates the antagonists and remedies the problem.

Chad

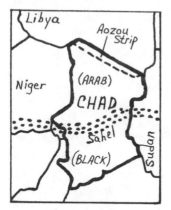

Landlocked Chad is one of the most impoverished nations on Earth. Like Sudan, it encompasses a Moslem north and a Black Christian/animist south united with each other by mutual hatred. In 1935, its senseless boundaries were arbitrarily drawn by the colonial French, who controlled Chad, and the colonial Italians, who controlled Libya. After World War II, Italy lost its empire and the British occupied Libya until independence in 1951. The British redrew the Chad/Libya border placing the Aozou strip, including the mineral-rich Tibesti mountains, in Chad instead of Libya.

Since France's relinquishment of its colonial empire in Africa in 1960, Chad has been wracked by a series of civil wars and periods of unrest extending to the present. French troops have period-ically returned to stabilize the political scene. The Aozou strip is a much fought-over prize which has triggered repeated wars and skirm-ishes between Chad and Libya. Its rich uranium deposits are coveted by Libya who may have motives other than simple commercial exploitation—development of a nuclear bomb.

It appears Chad will suffer perennial turmoil until it establishes autonomy for its two primary ethnic groups—one north of the Sahel, the other south. Like Sudan, Chad needs to create two new nations by drawing an east-west boundary along the Sahel (see map). Numer-ous tribal entities would remain within each new nation, but they'd stand a much better chance for coexistence, representation and pros-perity within a relatively common ethnic framework. A permanent boundary between Chad and Libya also needs to be formally estab-lished and agreed upon once and for all.

Besides the Sahel and its misplaced international borders, other parts of Africa have persistent boundary problems. Scrutiny continues to highlight ethnic differences as the primary cause of conflict and we suggest creation of new borders along natural ethnic boundaries to settle age-old disputes. Following are analyses of other African regions on which to base our proposition.

Western Sahara

Formerly called Spanish Sahara, this strip of desert along the Atlantic Ocean has been overrun and coveted for centur-ies. Its commercial value lies in rich phosphate deposits and some of the world's most pro-ductive offshore fishing grounds. In recent history, the Western Sahara has been alter-nately conquered and fought over by Morocco, Algeria,

Mauritania and Spain. The primary inhabitants of this barren, sparsely populated desert region are the Saharawis who, like the Kurds of the Mideast, are a nation without a country. The Saharawis occupy four countries—Morocco, Algeria, Mauritania and Western Sahara— but have autonomy nowhere.

We suggest one of two solutions to the turmoil in Western Sahara: the formal establishment of recognized international bound- aries legitimizing the Western Sahara as the Saharawis' homeland; or a form of limited autonomy, less than full independence, whereby Western Sahara might be a protectorate of Morocco while achiev- ing a higher level of governmental and commercial sophistication preparatory to full independence.

South Africa

The entire southern portion of Africa must be considered within the context of its inescapable dependency on South Africa. South Africa is the greatest economic dynamo on the African continent— the commercial lifeline for Malawi, Angola, Zambia, Namibia, Botswana, Mozambique, Zimbabwe, Tanzania and beyond. South African food exports sustain these countries, and its railroad system brings their products to markets and ports.

Like the Mideast and oil, conflict is heightened tremendously in South Africa by the presence of the world's largest known reserves of gold, chromium, platinum, vanadium, manganese and andalusite, plus large deposits of diamonds, asbestos and antimony. Half the world's annual gold output comes from South Africa. Thus, it becomes strategically important as well as politically expedient to settle conflict in South Africa, one of the world's hot spots. Before suggesting solutions to South Africa's explosive problems, a basic understanding of its history is required.

The earliest known inhabitants of South Africa were the Bush- men and Hottentots, scattered nomadic hunters comparable in some ways to North America's indigenous Indian population. In the 17th century, the Dutch established the first white colony at Cape Town, and its descendants are the Afrikaaners. Although a few scattered

Bantu (Black) tribes lived in what is modern day Transvaal Province prior to the 17th century, mass migrations of Bantus from eastern Africa to South Africa didn't begin until about the time the Dutch arrived. The Zulu and Xhosa tribes were the primary Bantu tribes then, as today, and were often bitter rivals, as now.

During the Napoleonic wars in the early 19th century, the British annexed Dutch South Africa. Just as in North America, South Africa's indigenous tribes could be considered as having a claim to the land, but in both cases the sheer mass of immigrants smothered once and for all any notions of proprietorship. For all practical purposes, setting aside the Bushmen and Hottentots, the overwhelming majority of the residents in today's South Africa—the Bantus and the Whites—*both* have legitimate claims to South Africa.

During the 19th century there was ongoing conflict *between* Whites (Afrikaaners vs. English), Blacks (primarily Zulus vs. Xhosas) and Whites vs. Blacks. Shaka, the Zulu king who established an empire based on what is modern day Natal and Transvaal Provinces, is renowned as one of the most bloodthirsty tyrants in history. He's estimated to have killed a million people in the 12 years before his assassination. The Bantu tribes were finally defeated and brought under control by the British in 1879.

In 1834, a group of Afrikaaner farmers (Boers) upset with British rule, trekked from the Cape to Natal and established a new colony which the British promptly annexed. Seeking autonomy, the Boers then trekked onward to the interior and established two small republics for themselves, the Orange Free State and the South African Republic (Transvaal). Diamonds and gold were discovered and the British, in the person of Cecil Rhodes who had already established British colonies to the north which he named Rhodesia, decided it must expand the empire by once again annexing Boer republics— the mineral rich Transvaal and Orange Free State. This imperialist empire-building angered the Boers whose toleration ended in 1899 when they attacked the British. The besieged British finally won after 200,000 troop reinforcements (among them a young soldier by the name of Winston Churchill) were rushed in. The Boer Wars

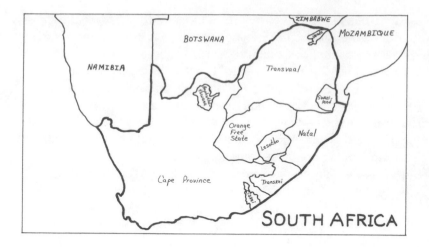

were costly with nearly 22,000 British and 7,000 Afrikaaners dead. Worst of all, the British rounded up tens of thousands of Afrikaaner civilians, including women and children, and put them in history's first concentration camps, where 18,000-28,000 died of disease in deplorable conditions. About 20,000 Blacks were also killed in the war which lasted until 1902. In 1910, South Africa was established by federating all Afrikaaners, British and Blacks within present-day borders.

Although the practice of racial separation goes all the way back to South Africa's colonial origins, apartheid wasn't formally established until 1948. Under apartheid, South Africa's population was deemed to consist of 10 separate Black nations or Bantustans (covering 13.6% of the country's land area, one White nation (four provinces—Cape, Natal, Orange Free State and Transvaal—consisting of 80% of the territory, including all the best farmland, the mines and the cities), one Indian Bantustan and one Colored Bantustan. Six of the Black Bantustans are self-governing, but don't want full independence. Four of the Black Bantustans—Transkei, Bophuthatswana, Venda and Ciskei—have been proclaimed independent, though they have tremendous problems and none are recognized by any nation besides South Africa and the other three. These four independents are considering a return to non-independent status, since they would qualify for protection by the White South Africa Defense Forces during these times of increasing Black infighting. Transkei, a Xhosa state, is as corrupt and tyrannical as any dictatorship in Africa and has been in a virtual state of war with Ciskei.

Besides the above, four completely independent states, having the characteristics of Bantustans, exist within or adjacent to South African and have historically close ties: Lesotho, which is entirely surrounded by South Africa; Swaziland, between South Africa and Mozambique; Botswana, to the northwest; and Namibia, a former South African protectorate which became independent in 1990. The first three were former British protectorates never ceded to South Africa. Botswana has considerable mineral resources and is the most independent of the four.

Under apartheid, Blacks in South Africa have a higher standard of living, are better educated and have better health care than Blacks anywhere in Africa. However, an unbridgeable gap still exists between them and the standard of living of South Africa's Whites. For decades Blacks were employed in the mines as transient labor at unchanging salaries and with no pensions. That's all changing as unprecedented milestones are being reached on the road to dismantling apartheid. At the present rate, Whites will soon be just another tribe within the extremely factious mosaic of African jungle politics.

However, Whites will continue to be southern Africa's most important tribe and acceptance or rejection of their leadership will seal the fate of all Africans south of the Congo for generations to come. Apartheid aside, the fact remains that White tribes have created the economic and technological infrastructure which exists as the only real hope for all tribes to uplift themselves from primitive squalor to a civilized future. Unfortunately, the racist reverberations emanating from some of the Black community in South Africa these days (and from the Frontline States over the years) isn't reassuring.

Black Africa's greatest fear *should* be that ethnic (tribal) rivalries will degenerate to their timeless historical levels of genocide and fratricide. Undeniably, there's a groundswell of this very thing underway as Nelson Mandela, a Xhosa, appears unable to curtail attacks on Zulus by young ANC radicals while Zulu Chief Buthelezi is unable to stop counter-attacks. The potential exists for one of the bloodiest tribal wars in African history and the victor, with an unquenchable thirst for blood, might turn on Whites and all other tribes. The fire could easily spread and ignite all of southern Africa, forcing a suicidal plunge backwards into the past. That's not a prediction, just a theoretical possibility.

To some, South Africa symbolizes all the evils of both colonialism and capitalism in today's world. Blacks, the Third World, and the left wing generally, mercilessly hold up racism embodied in a rapidly disappearing apartheid system as proof of the horrible sins committed by Whites. While we in no way condone apartheid, the fact is that a deathly *double standard* exists *among Black Africans* in which Black killings by Blacks are *accepted*, but Black killings by Whites are grounds for international condemnation, sanctions and terrorism. Over the past 30 years, approximately 5,000-6,000 Blacks have been killed in South Africa, the vast majority of them by Blacks themselves. Because of *intense media bias*, most of the world is not aware of the unreported atrocities which occurred elsewhere in Africa during this same time frame. Millions died in the Sahel by murder or through genocidal starvation of Blacks by Blacks. 100,000 members of the Hutu tribe in Burundi were massacred in 1972 by rival Tutsi tribesmen. As recently as August 1988, another 22,000 Hutu and Tutsi tribesmen were massacred in Burundi, but few have even heard of Burundi, much less a massacre there. Few remember that two million people were killed in the Black Biafran Civil War. But, just mention the Sharpeville massacre in which 69 South African Blacks were killed by Whites, and the reaction is tantamount to revolution. Whatever happened to perspective?

Racial problems have been so totally blown out of proportion in South Africa that the world fails to see the greatest threat is a communist ANC drive to grab power. The ANC (political arm of the Xhosa tribe which seeks the armed overthrow of the White government) is *not* even the dominant South African tribe. The Zulu tribe is six times bigger. Yet the ANC violently opposes power sharing with the Zulus (who want a peaceful transition to power sharing with the Whites) in a fashion that is at *least* as discriminatory as any acts ever attributed to Whites by Blacks.

The concept of Bantustans or tribal homelands is inherently sensible and satisfies the all-important need for ethnic autonomy. It has worked best in Bantustan-like Botswana, which has received much help and guidance from South Africa. It has essentially failed in the 10 Black Bantustans within South Africa, but that's due in great part to the lack of a sophisticated economic and social infrastructure that would exist under a non-apartheid system. Autonomous tribal homelands need to be established for the Zulu and Xhosa tribes. Equitable boundaries for such homelands should be satisfactorily determined by the White and Black tribes of South Africa, not outsiders. A totally "off the cuff" example: Transvaal might be a suitable Xhosa homeland, Natal a Zulu homeland, Orange Free State an Afrikaaner homeland and Cape Province a homeland for Coloreds, Indians, Indigenous tribes and British. This is oversimplified and would require a great deal of study and negotiations by the people of South Africa to determine.

Regardless of where homelands boundaries are drawn, it's vitally important to retain all homelands under the federal framework of the existing government system which functions well—it just needs to include Blacks as well as Whites. The multi-racial government needs to be initially guided by Whites as they, virtually alone in all of southern Africa, have the experience to make it work. The only lasting solution may be a realignment of autonomous tribal boundaries in conjunction with the dismantling of apartheid's racist foundations. We've already proposed changing old boundaries or creating new ones to resolve conflict in other regions of Africa, but nowhere is the future of the continent more critical than in South Africa, the major technological and industrial nerve center of the entire continent. It's absolutely vital to create formal and acceptable boundaries fully honoring South Africa's ethnic diversity. The survival and well-being of millions of people in many countries is at stake, not only in South Africa.

Angola

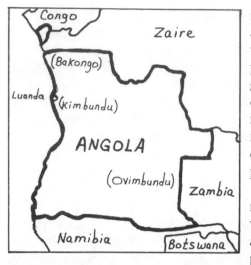

Present-day Angola is a classic third world disaster created by mixing virtually every volatile political ingredient into a giant cocktail. To get a grip on Angola's predicament requires a short review of its history—including the devastating effect of superpower meddling.

Portugal began colonizing Angola in 1575, with the establishment of a fort at Luanda, the present capital. The Portuguese were incompetent and cruel and sent about 3 million slaves to their New World colony of Brazil during their rule. Beginning in the 1950s, Portugal settled about 300,000 Portuguese peasants in Angola, and about 250,000 in Mozambique, hoping to build more Brazils in Africa. However, independence movements arose all across Africa in the 1960s, including Angola, and their plan collapsed.

Three Angolan independence groups entered the political picture in the 1960s, and they were divided along tribal and ideological lines. The Marxist MPLA (Movimento Popular de Libertacao de Angola), with Cuban and Soviet support, was founded in 1956 by the exiled Dr. Agostinho Neto and established itself in Zaire, far from its Kimbundu tribal power base around Luanda. The FNLA (Frente Nacional de Libertacao de Angola), with Zairean and US support, was founded in 1960 by Holden Roberto and also established itself in Zaire. However, its Bakongo tribal power base was in northern Angola adjacent to Zaire where the dominant tribe is also the Bakongo. UNITA (Uniao Nacional para a Independencia Total de Angola), the third independence group, was formed in 1966 when a dissatisfied FNLA leader, the charismatic Dr. Jonas Savimbi, broke away and established his own power base in eastern Angola among Angola's largest tribe the Ovimbundu. Savimbi received primary support from the US and South Africa.

Portugal maintained control over Angola during the 1960s and early 1970s, and none of the rebel independence movements presented a serious threat. However, Portugal was having serious control problems in its other African colonies of Guinea and Mozambique, and the effort exacted an unsustainable drain on Portugal's resources. Portugal's colonial umbilical cord snapped in April 1974 when leaders of a successful military coup in Lisbon announced that all Portuguese colonies would be granted independence. In Angola, the Portuguese prepared to set up a transitional coalition government consisting of the three independence groups, MPLA, FNLA and UNITA. Leaders of the three groups were called to Lisbon where they signed the Alvor agreement providing for the establishment of a coalition government upon independence in November 1975, 400 years after the Portuguese first arrived in Angola. From that point on, events really began deteriorating.

Almost immediately, civil war broke out among the coalition partners, with little effort on the part of any for mutual cooperation. Simultaneously, the USSR was in the process of dramatically expanding its global empire and influence into Africa and soon massive arms shipments and tens of thousands of Cuban and Soviet troops were supplied to the MPLA. The US, fresh from defeat in Vietnam, was reluctant to get involved immediately in another foreign war. However, Henry Kissinger was determined the US could also ill afford another defeat, so the CIA began secretly funneling arms to the FNLA and UNITA through Zaire and Zambia. The US Congress passed a law in December 1975 forbidding further assistance to UNITA, but it was too late; by now Angola was well on its way to becoming a third world battlefield for the clash by proxy of super-power titans. The Soviets did not stop their assistance to the Marxist MPLA, so with unbridled Soviet and Cuban support, the MPLA soon dominated Angola. The FNLA disintegrated, UNITA retreated into the bush and all 300,000 Portuguese settlers departed.

Although the MPLA became the officially recognized government of Angola, UNITA regrouped and with South African and later renewed US support under Reagan, it controlled huge sections of southern, central and eastern Angola. It established an enviable infrastructure for a rebel independence movement, replete with schools, hospitals and industry, and was able to partially support itself with profits from diamond mining. UNITA launched rebel attacks on the MPLA at will, and without Cuban and Soviet support, the Marxist MPLA government in Luanda would have collapsed. Ironically, in addition to $1 billion in weapons supplied annually by the Soviets during the mid-1980s, the MPLA was able to augment its income with profits from oil exports by US-based Chevron and Texaco, while their opposition (UNITA) was receiving support from the US government.

The stalemated situation in Angola was building to a climax in 1988, as all-out war threatened between UNITA and South Africa on one side, and Soviet-supported Angola and Cuba on the other. Then, an historical turning point of the 20th century arrived just in the nick of time, when the Soviets suddenly realized they must pay the price for decades of "imperial over-reach." Their empire began crumbling within and without; they were forced to partially abandon Afghanistan, and they began abandoning or drastically cutting their commitments to all Marxist client states, including Angola. The stage was set for superpower agreement to stop interfering in Angolan tribal matters that shouldn't have concerned them in the first place. The Soviets pulled out, all Cubans are scheduled to be out by July 1991, and the US is only supporting UNITA to the extent necessary to counter MPLA aggression.

Except for oil produced by US companies, the entire economy of MPLA-controlled Angola has collapsed and the currency is worthless. Virtually all trade is on a barter basis. It's believed Angola's standard of living, life expectancy, infant mortality rates and health services are worse now than in the early 19th century. The *International Index of Human Suffering*, prepared by the Population Crisis Committee in Washington, ranks Angola as the world's second most miserable place behind Mozambique, another former Portuguese colony. Things can't get much worse, but we believe a rare opportunity may soon exist to draw new boundaries to set the stage for a long, but lasting recovery in Angola.

We mentioned earlier that the three original Angolan independence movements were created along tribal and ideological lines. It's probable the MPLA's Marxist ideology will cease to exist once Soviet and Cuban support are gone. However, its Kimbundu tribal identity will remain. UNITA, political arm of the Ovimbundu tribe, controls major portions of Angola, and will likely conquer the MPLA in the power vacuum left by the Cubans' departure. Will UNITA follow historical African tribal practices of slaughtering adversaries or will uncharacteristic benevolence and tolerance be extended? Numerous attempts have been made by outsiders to get UNITA and the MPLA to negotiate elections and power sharing, but such talks have always collapsed. Unfortunately, high risk exists for a massive blood bath once all superpower influence is gone.

Perhaps a last chance to avoid such bloodshed is by creation of new borders separating major tribes along historical ethnic/tribal lines and formalizing and enforcing those borders at something like UN level. The resultant tribal homelands should be guaranteed "near sovereignty" in a democratic Angola or complete "new nation" status within the international order. Angola is mostly devoid of racial problems; however, ethnic/tribal rivalries are so intense that any attempts to meld tribes together would be doomed. Instead of trying to decree the impossible merging of centuries of conflict, culture and tradition, the obvious solution is to create natural, ethnic borders and respect them in order to stop the killing. It may astound the world to discover that creation of borders demarcating natural and historical ethnic entities will lead to peace, prosperity and mutual respect.

Mozambique

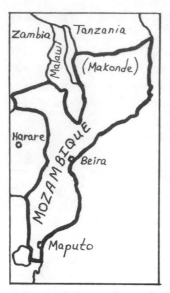

Striking historical parallels exist between Angola and Mozambique and the common denominators are the Portuguese and Soviets. Mozambique, like Angola, was colonized by Portugal in the 16th century, neglected until the 20th, and became independent in 1975. Also like Angola and many other African nations, Mozambique made the disastrous mistake of adopting Marxism.

Civil war broke out following 1975 independence and an estimated 400,000 people have since been killed or starved. (Virtually all war deaths were caused by Blacks killing Blacks.) The *International Index of Human Suffering* ranks Mozambique as the world's most miserable country, with half to two-thirds of its 14 million population dependent on international relief for survival. An estimated 1.5 million Mozambicans are refugees in neighboring countries.

Frelimo (Frente Libertacao de Mocambique), founded in 1962, was the first independence movement and the political arm of the Makonde tribe of northern Mozambique. Upon independence from Portugal in 1975, Frelimo assumed power and moved its leadership to the capital of Maputo in extreme southern Mozambique, faraway from its Makonde power base (northern Mozambique is as far from Maputo as Stockholm is from Rome). Like the MPLA in Angola, the USSR began supplying Marxist Frelimo with substantial weaponry immediately after independence. Frelimo responded by proclaiming its hostility to South African and Rhodesia and cutting off the Beira railway, landlocked Rhodesia's lifeline to the sea which ran from Salisbury (now Harare) to the port city of Beira in Mozambique. Rhodesia retaliated in 1976 by forming Renamo (Mozambique

National Resistance), consisting of Blacks and Whites based in Rhodesia and Mozambique.

With Rhodesia's independence (and name change to Zimbabwe) in 1980, Renamo moved its base to South Africa, and the intensity of conflict grew. The outlawed South African Communist ANC (Africa National Congress) set up a base in Maputo alongside the Marxist Frelimo. In succeeding years, Renamo and South African security forces wreaked such havoc among Frelimo and the ANC that Mozambique's Frelimo President Samora Machel agreed to sign the Nkomati accord in 1984. The accord stipulated that South Africa would stop supporting Renamo if Frelimo would stop supporting the ANC. Once the accord was formalized, Renamo relocated to Mozambique, where it continued fighting, ostensibly without South Africa's help, against Frelimo, and now controls up to 80% of the Mozambican countryside.

President Machel was killed in a plane crash in 1986, and his Frelimo successor is Joaquim Chissano. With USSR economic collapse and drastic cuts in Soviet aid, Chissano is reluctantly making friendly overtures to the West. While the Frelimo government isolated in Maputo barely hangs on to power, Renamo, led by Alfonso Dhlakama from the tiny Ndau tribe, enjoys the support of most of Mozambique's people. As in Angola, attempts have been made to establish negotiations, hold elections and share power. Similarly, all attempts have failed, and the downfall of Frelimo gets ever closer just as it does for the MPLA in Angola. When Frelimo's fall comes, odds are great that it will be accompanied by a tribal blood bath.

Once again, solutions involving the creation of new borders and possibly new nations scream for attention. Frelimo should abandon Marxism and the futility of trying to rule a country twice the size of California and return to its faraway northern homeland. An official and mutually acceptable border should be created between the historical Makonde homeland to the north and the Makua, Mozambique's largest tribe, whose traditional homeland occupies central Mozambique. Although Remano's Dhlakama is from a small tribe, he has the overwhelming popular support needed to lead all tribes under a national umbrella. The success of his leadership would depend on whether tribal leaders are prepared to respect each other's autonomy. Following Kenyan President Jomo Kenyatta's death in 1978, Daniel arap Moi, who is from a small tribe, effectively led that country for many years. Unfortunately, President Moi has become enamored with power in recent years and brutally subjugates all political opponents.

Summary

We've briefly analyzed many ongoing conflicts across the African continent, but many more have gone unmentioned. We've offered obvious and workable solutions: the formal creation of new borders and respect for ethnically autonomous territories. If various homelands wish to unite under a national umbrella for purposes of trade and commerce, currency, etc., this arrangement need not violate their autonomy. Africa contains many of the world's largest nations—arbitrarily and forcefully created by colonial empires during the twilight of a bygone era. It's *high noon in Africa*'s history and urgent decisions need to be taken and changes made if Africa's people are to have a future. Failure to act means millions more people will die unnecessarily and additional millions will suffer from starvation or as refugees.

Chapter 10

Latin America

Although Latin America is stricken with debt and poverty, it's far ahead of Africa in terms of possessing sensible borders. While post-colonial Africa is just awakening to the nightmare of ill-conceived borders, Latin America finds most of its borders are approximately in the right place. Latin America has many economic and governmental problems, but few border problems.

However, there is one area in Latin America screaming for independent new nation status, and it's gigantic—the entire Amazon River Basin, or Amazonia. Amazonia is a massive, remote, undeveloped backwater that, in some respects, is less understood than the surface of the moon. Many of its inhabitants are primitive people, and it contains thousands of species of plants and animals not even yet identified. The potential mineral, medicinal and timber resources of Amazonia are inestimable. The fact that it's the world's largest tropical rain forest and the globe's major air purifier lends critical scientific and environmental importance to Amazonia. It constitutes nearly half the total land area of Brazil, a nation with overwhelming economic and administrative problems and little time to concentrate on Amazonia.

A major conference should be convened involving all South American nations bordering on Amazonia for the purpose of granting independence and establishing its borders. The Amazon River Basin extends into portions of Colombia, Ecuador, Peru and Bolivia, and all these nations should be asked to contribute land to Amazonia, in addition to Brazil. If political obstacles are insurmountable, Brazil

should grant independence to Amazonia while other national borders remain unchanged. A logical place for a capital would be Manaus, centrally located on the Amazon River.

The first step by Amazonia's new government should be to establish a team of scientific experts from academia and private industry to advise it on environmentally sound and sensible development of its vast resources. Private industry should be invited to participate in the development of Amazonia under guidelines and parameters established by the government and its advisory team. Amazonia is vital to the global environment and much too important to be left to remote and distracted government officials in Brazil. Amazonia independence would place responsibility directly on the people of the Amazon River Basin for conservation and safe and profitable development. It would be in the best interest of everyone on Planet Earth.

PS: Not incidentally, this would save the Yanomani Indians, who have been killed & dispossessed via mindless exploitation.

Border Disputes

For such a big continent, there are amazingly few border disputes. They include:

1. Argentina/Chile (Fireland: Vatican mediated).
2. Venezuela/Guyana (about one-third of Guyana's eastern part is claimed by Venezuela, with no solution in sight, and Guyana's leaders unable or unwilling to exploit promising ideas).

Chapter 11

The 700-Year-Old Example of Switzerland

I n 1291 three liberty-minded citizens representing the inhabitants of three valleys in the center of Europe's Alps promised to help each other to fend off the imposition of foreign rule, taxes and judges. They laid the basis for one of the most durable experiments in nation-building: Europe's multi-cultured Switzerland, which gives birth to four of Europe's most important rivers (Rhine, Rhone, Po and Donau). Let's look at what these Founding Fathers agreed upon way back in 1291. It may interest those seeking inspiration for addressing nationality problems, and also to those trying to find out what may be leading Switzerland off its original successful track. Here's a translation of Switzerland's basic document:

SWISS FEDERAL PACT—August 1, 1291

In the name of God, the Almighty, amen. It is accomplishing an honorable and beneficial action for the public well-being to confirm, in the established forms, the conventions aimed at peace and security.

[1] Let it be known to everybody, considering the prevailing evil and in order to better defend and maintain in their integrity their families and their property, that the People of the valleys of Uri, Schwyz and Unterwalden, in good faith, have pledged to assist each other with help, with advice and with all favors, persons and goods, inside their valleys and beyond, with all

their power and resourcefulness, against all and against any-body nourishing bad intentions or who committed a crime, an offense or an injustice against any one or more of them, or concerning their property.

[2]   Each Community has pledged to come to the aid of the other, whenever that is necessary, to help against and, in as much as that is indicated, at its own costs, to resist and revenge the attacks of ill-intended people, having previously made such an oath which is herewith effectively renewed.

[3]   notwithstanding each person's right, to the best of its abilities, to be obedient and helpful to his [or her] master.

[4]   After joint consultations, we have also unanimously agreed, set and ordered that the People of the above-named valleys will under no circumstances receive or accept a judge who is not one of us [i.e., a resident and citizen], or who has bought his judgeship with money or any kind of favor in any way.

[5]   Should a difference occur among any of the Confederates, it is incumbent on those who carry the most respect to intervene and appease the difference with the most effective means they consider appropriate. All other Confederates shall unite against the party which refuses the [arbitration] sentence.

[6]   Also they have agreed to the following rules to be observed: he who with intent and without being provoked caused somebody's death shall, as is indicated by the infamy of this crime and unless he can show his innocence, be put to death upon being caught, and he shall never be allowed to return if he escapes. Those giving shelter and protection to such an evil person shall be banned from these valleys until the Con-federates may have called them back.

[7]   He who with intent, by day or in the dark of the night, set fire to the property of a Confederate shall have lost forever his rights as a member of our Communities, and he who shelters and protects this offender shall in our valleys compensate the injured.

[8]   Moreover, the property in the valleys of any Confederate who, by way of robbery or otherwise, inflicted any damage on the property of any other Confederate, shall be sequestrated in as much as is needed to compensate said damage in due course.

[9]   Also, nobody among ourselves shall seize the other's property without a valid public title or a guarantee, and then only with a special authorization from his [the competent] judge.

[10]   Each one shall be obedient to his judge and, if that becomes necessary, shall indicate the judge of the valley which he is prepared to recognize.

[11]   Whoever opposes or refuses obedience to a [competent] court and thus causes damage to anyone among us, shall be liable to render satisfaction which is to be enforced by all other Confederates.

[12]   Should war or a conflict break out among the Confederates and one party refuses to respect the law and customs, all other Confederates shall protect the other party.

[13]   The above-mentioned laws, set as they are in the interest and for the benefit of all, shall, God permitting, remain in force forever. In witness whereof the present act, set up at the request of the aforesaid, has been validated with the affixed seals of the above-mentioned Communities and valleys. Done at the beginning of August in the year of the Lord 1291.

Some wish to continue talking of Switzerland as Heidiland, an idealized chocolate and cuckoo-clock paradise somewhere between Sweden and Swaziland. But others may start to look at this *nation-through-willpower Confederation* as a valid indication of the interests of differing communities—and the corresponding rules—which can best be served on a higher, a confederated level. Thus never losing sight of the well-being of their residents as the *litmus test for the legitimacy* of both the communities and the confederation's actions and inactions. They may discover the virtues of referenda and people's assemblies (Landsgemeinde) where laws and regulations must be "sold" to the "voter" in his presence at a public place, as is still the case.

Other readers will also be fascinated by the slow but steady evolution of Switzerland's sovereign political entities, i.e., the cantons, some of which, like Geneva, assertively call themselves Republics. Some continue to split, like the Canton of Berne which is transferring sovereignty over part of its territory to the Canton of Basel-Landschaft and which, ten years ago, gave birth to the Republic and Canton of Jura.

Others, notably the Republic and Canton of Geneva, are moving toward more independence, and this might benefit the rest of Switzerland, particularly regarding its relations with the rest of Europe and, while it lasts, the EC. It recalls the case of Switzerland's unique UN vote (staying out, that is). And it is again, more glaringly, the case with regard to its relations with the EC.

Modern Switzerland, in 1848, was largely re-modeled after the United States 1776 Constitution. It managed to survive unscathed, the tempests that ravaged Europe in the first half of this century. This was due to its policy of *permanent armed neutrality* dating back to 1575 when, in the battle of Marignano, Swiss soldiers of fortunes fought each other in different camps. An agrarian state until the last century, the evolution of *its society and economy is seen to have benefited decisively from the influx of enterprising foreigners* from its major European and American trading partners who were encouraged to settle by way of (in theory still valid) friendship, commerce and establishment treaties.

However, the basis of *Switzerland's enviable prosperity, in recent years, has been undermined by official neglect of individual rights and, notably, of fundamental sovereignty and fiscal principles.* Pressures of neighboring governments and, particularly, American officials working in power vacuums, have been allowed to wreak havoc on the libertarian structures and laws of the Swiss (e.g., the growing *lex americana*, e.g., laws against insider trading, money laundering, and export controls). This has become manifest notably with recent *US court decisions*.

Please excuse this further divergence form the book's theme.

Aside from exposing some useful realities, it serves to warn that even in small, well-run states, vigilance is essential to preserve individual liberty. Moreover it shows how BIG nations, especially in superpower size, tend to (& always have) pushed their rules down the throats of other nations.

Thus bigness is *an evil per se*, as it always represents **power**, & power will always be **used**. In theory, if every nation were the *same* size or power, nobody could force their guidelines upon other countries. These days, the US enforces its *lex americana* on the world. Imposing its standards, supposedly for the "good" of all. But much wrong is done in the name of goodness. Not all agree with US standards on bank practices, taxation, tax enforcement, tax punishment, money reporting requirements, limits of money transporting, use of cash restrictions, dismissal of the gold standard, drug enforcement, boarding foreign ships in international waters by US coastguard officers, tax avoidance classified as tax evasion, insider trading (although without definition), drug criminalization, ban on secret bank accounts, no right to undisclosed assets, burden of proof of crime on the accused not the accuser, etc., etc.

Yet the US is imposing all or most of its standards on every nation, even though other nations have laws of their own that are quite different. Often opposite. So, big *is* bad because big is power & power will always be put to use. It's often a case of "I'm going to hit you for your own good."

Chapter 12

Western Europe

There is a first-glance tendency to think that West Europe is pretty much OK, borderwise, *as is.* And for most of it that's true.

But if you take it country by country, you find there are quite a few in need of changes. Let's list them:

Spain

The Basque country has been a sore point in Spain for a very long time. Killings take place routinely, which proves the problem is serious and must be addressed. Spain is big enough to let the Basques have their own nation, in my opinion. Autonomy without nationhood might suffice, but it should be put to a vote. Let all Spain vote and let the Basques vote be counted separately. I would hazard a guess that Spain as a whole would vote in favor of it by some 55% and the Basques would favor it by 90%. If the result were along these lines, clearly a separation is called for if the vote result was only 30% in Spain and 40% in Basque, then it would be a dead issue and it would probably stop the violence, for they would have had their "day in court" and discovered the public was NOT with them. Either way it would be progressive.

Many Spaniards would feel I was negligent if I didn't bring up the case for separatism for Barcelona. They have always felt superior to Madrid, and have a very strong local patriotism. I suggest, before a national referendum is held, a ballot should take place first just within greater Barcelona, or Catalonia. If it was say

70% or more in favor, then there is a case for holding a national referendum.

France

No change needed, in my opinion, in mainland France. Offshore there are separatist movements which don't concern us here. Except to say the Corsican separatists are especially vocal, have resorted to terrorism in mainland France and kidnappings in Corsica. My advice would be to hold a referendum in Corsica to see if a clear majority favor nationhood. If it was less than a 60% favorable vote the issue would be declared void. If it was 60% or more, then a referendum in mainland France would be a consideration. A simple majority vote here should be required for the separatists. Tourists are afraid to visit Corsica because of the kidnapping or terrorist risk. It should be dealt with by ballot, so the issue can be resolved one way or the other. It shouldn't really matter *which* way it goes, as long as, it represents a clear majority desire. France is suffering more by this pointless, ignoring of the matter, than it would from holding a poll and either generously granting independence or proving it unwanted.

Holland

No change need, in my opinion.

Belgium

There is a case for two nations here since there is much bitterness over the language question. It's French-speaking Waloons in the south versus Dutch speaking Flemish in the north. It is a constant irritant, and it apparently won't go away—if it hasn't in all these years. As with Spain, I think a national referendum is called for. If the vote to have separate nations passes by, say 60%, then divorce proceedings should begin. If the vote is under 50% then it will be dead. If it is 55% it should be put aside and done again in 5 years to see if opinions change. But I think 60% is probably needed for so big a decision. A mere 51% for example would hardly be conclusive, and could result from clever electioneering or TV tactics by one side.

Luxembourg

No change needed, in my opinion.

Andorra

No change needed, in my opinion.

Germany

After the recent reunification of the two Germanys, I think it is safe to presume no further changes are called for. Certainly the old issue of the Polish border should not be dug up again, even though the case is not as black and white for status quo as the untutored public believes. But public relations-wise it is best left alone.

Austria

No change needed, in my opinion. There has been talk of an East & West Austria at times but it doesn't seem serious. If some think it should be serious, then they should petition for a referendum. If not enough signatures are obtained by petition then it would not deserve an election.

Switzerland

Some internal changes may occur, as referred to elsewhere in this book, like Geneva becoming a republic. That idea has a life of its own, with merit, and I hope it comes to a vote. I have no idea whether the vote would be positive or negative. But it would not harm Switzerland either way. Only *not voting* is harmful, anywhere.

United Kingdom

There has been controversy and even killings, over the decades, regarding nationhood for Scotland and Wales and Northern Ireland. Certainly each area is a different personality. They are NOT *English*. I have lived in England for many years and claim to know the situation with the objectivity of a relative outsider, and having been married to both a Scot and an English girl. I've been an Anglophile most of my life (although I decry its move into Orwellian legal & tax practices), so I speak with considerable experience. It is my firm belief that the issue of separate nationhoods for Scotland, Wales, and Northern Ireland, should be put to a vote. As with Belgium, I think a 60% majority should be required for nationhood. The vote should, as with Spain, be taken separately for each area and also an amalgamated total. Both the area in question and the grand total should be a 60% majority. It might even be wise to consider a demand that the area in question should be 70% while only 60% is enough for the grand total of all areas.

Some referendums are legally binding. Some are merely persuasive evidence for legislators to take account of, or as back up for independence movements.

Monaco

No change is needed, in my opinion.

Italy

Ah, here we have a clear case of a crying need for change. Everyone admits the Northern Italian has nothing in common with the far Southern Italian. And all agree the national bureaucracy doesn't function. Neither does the postal system, the tax system, and more. The food works. And so does the beauty and the dispositions. But the country doesn't. Even the GNP is a figment of imagination because so much of it isn't counted, the portion from the free economy, the unregulated sector, the black economy, whatever you care to call it. I'm writing this page in Venice, which used to be a kingdom, and should be again. My friend Paolo Barozzi (whose family were Venetians for many generations) said the North of Italy is as different to the South as Moscow and Bombay. When I said Venezia should return to being the Republic of Venice, he agreed. It once dominated the culture of the known world. He says, Venice has more in common with New York City than nearby Milan.

Milan is a powerful economy and could easily be a nation unto itself, along with nearby Genoa & Turin and across to the French border. Certainly most of Italy would benefit from being cut off from Rome. Show me an Italian who disagrees with that! (except a Roman). Italy is ungovernable as is. Its had more elected government *changes* than any democracy in the world, by far. Governments keep falling. Italy would gain and grow if it were divided into perhaps 7 or 9 Republics. Don't say they would be too small. Tiny San Marino thrives in a corner pocket of Italy. There are dozens of nations much smaller than each of the 7-9 "new" Italian nations would be.

Each would be excited to work hard and prosper, if they felt their local area was their *own* "private" sovereign nation, without tax revenues going to Rome and without Roman bureaucrats coming to monitor them. It's hard to be patriotic when you know the Rome politicians are messing things up. Which is what most Italians feel. Which is why the Italians are the world's leading tax avoiders. Until recently, most Italians virtually refused to pay taxes or only token sums.

Separate status for: Florence (Tuscany), Milan/Genoa/Turin, Venice/Padua/Verona/Friuli-Venezia-Giulia, Rome Region (Latium, Abruzzi), Sicily, Sardinia, Naples—south (for example) would create a fresh surge of drive and affinity. It could be magical, in my view.

Whether Umbria and Marches went with Rome or Florence, and whether Trent went with Milan or Venice, and whether Bologna went with Florence or Milan or Venice, is for locals to debate, with hand gestures. Italians are wonderful, warm, friendly people.

I love them. They deserve a better deal. 7-9 new nations, all with Italian Dressing, would be that better deal, in my opinion. How to get it started? Again, via referendums. First in each sector, to see if the locals really want it. Then nationally, using the kind of guidelines I gave for Belgium and Spain and the UK. Any individual person can start a petition going. If it is easy to get signatures, it wins a place on the ballot. If it doesn't, it dies.

Portugal

No change needed that I am aware of. Readers may advise me if I'm mistaken.

Czechoslovakia

This nation pokes into both West & East Europe. The debate has gotten bitter, again with regards to the separatist movement for Slovaks to chop themselves off from the Czechs. I can't evaluate the rights and wrongs on each side but I know that any feud that is this intense and lasted this long is entitled to a referendum, along the lines I suggest above for Spain, Belgium, Italy. Unfortunately, the communists seem to be using the Slovaks cause to break up the union and establish a regime they can control. But referendums will determine the validity of the Slovak claims.

Norway

No change needed, in my opinion (but see the last chapter).

Sweden

No change needed but I have often wondered if Sweden would be less socialist if it got a new start, which a division would bring about.

Finland

No change needed, so far as I know.

Republic of Ireland

No change needed, in my opinion.

Denmark

No change needed, in my opinion.

Greece

Probably no change needed, but readers can tell me if they disagree for the sequel edition. Meantime, Greece & Turkey should resolve their border war in **Crete** via plebiscite. A vote by the people of Crete should be weighted heavy, with votes from Greece & Turkey weighted on a slightly lesser scale. It is grossly unfair to let Crete go unresolved year after year. If civilized man pretends to believe in democracy, he must let people vote for their futures.

Yugoslavia

I seemed to have subconsciously left the most delicate for last. There has been an unofficial civil war here for many weeks as this page is written. Unfortunately, President Bush is meddling in Yugo affairs (in late May, 1991) by: (1) threatening to withhold US aid if a Croat isn't elected president and (2) expressing support for Mr. Markovic's efforts "to hold Yugoslavia together." This is shades of Abraham Lincoln. Man has learned nothing, apparently, in all the intervening years. Mr. Bush, and certain others, who are unenlightened in my appraisal, apparently feel it is justified to kill an unspecified number of people RATHER than let certain sectors have independence. So, I must ask the old Civil War question all over again: what is so special about preserving the UNION? Whether it is Yugoslavia, the USSR, the USA, China, Canada, wherever. Such unions do indeed have certain merits, but at what point does it run out of merit if it starts to cost human lives? How many lives is a political union worth? Two lives? 10? 150? 5,000? In my opinion, the answer is: none.

The Yugo situation changes daily. At this moment, Serbia is suggesting a loose alliance of *separate sovereign nations.* That makes perfect sense, in my opinion. It is the most certain way to avoid bloodshed. What difference does it make if this area contains 1 or 2 or 6 separate nations? They will, I am certain, work in greater harmony if each has sovereign rights, than being forced to sleep in the same political bed.

Norman Stone, one of my favorite columnists, writes, in London's Sunday Times (May 12, 1991) that we should *recognize* the separate state of Croatia *at once.* He tells us Yugoslavia is an artificial state, like Iraq, created after World War I that has gone on to make problems for everyone. Norman Stone says endorsing Yugo separatism is their only way out of communism. Norman Stone says "we are talking about the end of World War I, finally, in many respects, especially for the artificially created states that are now being destroyed from within. It's happening in Iraq, the USSR & Yugoslavia." He says World War I began in Yugoslavia and maybe it is finally ending there.

And as with the Baltics, the fastest way to give deserving new nations, or old subjected nations, their independence, is to give them official diplomatic recognition. This starts the ball rolling and stops all the negativity of the past from causing new damage.

In Slovenia, they've already printed their own passports and money and plan to declare independence June 26, 1991, regardless of what the rest of Yugoslavia does. Last December its 2 million people voted overwhelmingly in referendum form to leave the patchwork of warring nationalities that for 73 years has been known as Yugoslavia. Slovenia, with only 8% of Yugo population, produces 25% of GNP, has offered to pay 25% of Yugo's debts. Slovenia needs recognition from the world now! I hope it will be forthcoming. Diplomatic cowardice is unbecoming of mankind in much of this century. We have seen enough of it, especially regarding the Baltics, not to mention the Hungarian uprising of 1956.

The Croatians voted in late May 1991 for independence, just as Slovenia had done 5 months earlier. The referendum was not legally binding, but it had symbolic importance. It gave support to those Croat leaders who are pressing for independence. The people are voicing their wishes. This is the kind of balloting that should take place wherever there are doubts about the future of any area, economically, financially, politically, socially.

Mihajlo Mihajlov, an author who spent seven years in Yugo jails as a dissident, says the West should not interpret reports of the military restoring law & order as good news. He says the army is communist run & they're itching to "restore order," meaning to restore communist control throughout Yugo. Mihajlov says people often confuse order with centralized military control. In the absence of a sound political order, a unified military is only an enforcer of tyranny. The chaos of free social life is not disorder; it is the natural way of change and adaptation. True order is built within and around the chaos, through democratic decision making processes and market structures. In nature scientists have found, order is always interlaced with chaos. The same is true in good govt., which establishes a framework of order for the fertile chaos of life, channeling it into mutually tolerable paths. Military suppression, by contrast, usually only causes chaos to fester underground.

Chapter 13

Homo Oeconomicus

Related key ideas, items and practical measures for statesmen and lawmakers, providing for the reappearance of the
citizen-entrepreneurs, the reanimation of homo oeconomicus
as the market's indispensable central driving force:

1. Shifting the powers from the bureaucracy back to the citizens

A nation's key responsibility—and source of legitimacy—i.e.,
its capacity to safeguard its citizen's pursuit of happiness, may be
met most effectively through genuine liberation of the citizen as its
only real sovereign.

2. Reintroduction of the original right to undisclosed private property

The burden of proof must be returned to the taxing authority,
i.e., the taxpayer's signature completing his tax return must no longer
be devalued by his current obligation to *substantiate* his figures with
bank records, salary statements, expense receipts, etc.

3. 10% maximum taxation rule

As a matter of sovereignty, the right to tax is inseparable from
the *obligation to protect the taxpayer against foreign taxation.* Also, if a
community—i.e., the structure embracing the resident family—with
its own resources, (its income from *its exclusive right to maximum 10%
direct taxes*), cannot efficiently provide a function which is indispensable for its survival, well-being, and pursuit of happiness, then responsibility for that function must be delegated to a correspondingly larger
political unit, such as a confederation, whose *exclusive indirect taxing*

authority may not exceed 10% of the value of the transacted goods and services.

> *Transition rule:* A community, reflecting its closer ties with the citizens (and thus its *naturally higher authority* in the hierarchy of a nation of sovereign citizens), shall have the (constitutionally enshrined) *right to negative taxation,* i.e., the right to unilaterally decide that its residents may *not* be subjected to direct tax filing obligations by *any* national or foreign authority, and that they may not be subject to national direct taxation beyond a speci-fied modest maximum.

4. *Recognizing and strengthening the citizens abroad and reinstating those abroad who have lost their citizenship (they are all economic ambassadors).*

5. *The low- and middle-level officials must be given the right to spend up to 50% **less** time on official business and to exercise independent functions compatible with, and not linked to his official duties—naturally with corres-ponding **cuts** in their salary and social benefits.*

The entrepreneurs constituting and playing the market—in both the West and the newly reborn democracies—increasingly find their freedom of economic action discouragingly reduced (if not voided) by uncomprehending, suspicious, non-cooperative officials. This could be changed by deliberately encouraging officials to become market players/entrepreneurs themselves and thus develop a more business-friendly mind set.

Chapter 14

India

Over half of the world's estimated five billion people live in Asia. Currently, India's population is 900 million—one-third of Asia's population and 18 % of the world's total. Although its land size is only a third of the USA's, India's increasingly restive population is four times greater. Plus, all the elements of violent ethnic conflict exist in India's giant curry pot of poverty and debt.

India is one of the world's oldest civilizations with Indus Valley excavations establishing a history at least 5000 years old. Aryan tribes invaded around 1500 BC and merged with earlier inhabitants to create classical Indian civilization. Islam gained a foothold between the 8th and 13th centuries and many of today's Indians steadfastly adhere to belief in Allah and the teachings of Mohammed. India came under control of the British empire in the 18th century and remained a colony until independence under Nehru in 1947. It's the world's largest democracy although great inequality exists under its caste social system. Fabian socialism provided the framework for today's floundering economic system and is probably the primary reason India has never escaped poverty and achieved prosperity.

Moslem East and West Pakistan were united with India under British rule. However they became autonomous after India's independence in 1947. East and West Pakistan subsequently became independent of each other and East Pakistan changed its name to Bangladesh. Both achieved independence from India to avoid war and reduce escalating ethnic conflict.

But, the autonomy process in India is far from finished as

evidenced by unpredictable surges of ethnic violence erupting like an awakening volcano. 83% of Indians belong to the Hindu religion and 11% are Moslems, while Christians, Sikhs and others make up the remaining 6%. Violent conflict has occasionally broken out between the majority Hindus and the Moslems and Sikhs. We now focus on some of the most critical areas of ethnic turmoil.

Sri Lanka

This independent island nation (unlike its giant northern neighbor) is an open prospering economy serving as a shining free-market example to all of Asia despite recent racial wars. However, it's a hot-bed of ethnic tension fatally linked to India's problems. The Tamils,

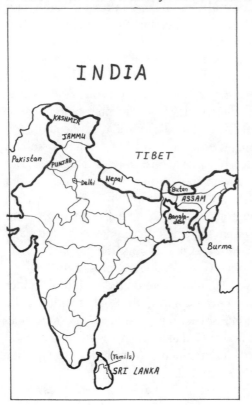

who occupy the north-eastern part of the island, have been fighting for secession from the majority Sinhalese. The Sinhalese were backed by Gandhi's Indian government during bloody fighting in recent years. Rajiv Gandhi's assassination during 1991 election campaigns was the result of a suicide bombing by a Tamil woman. A group called Operation Final Vengeance claimed responsibility saying it represented "minority groups in India and Sri Lanka who are seeking their *own homelands.*"

The Tamils, constituting 20% of the population, want secession from the 75% majority Sinhalese. However, many wealthy Tamils would not press for secession if the Sinhalese would simply grant the Tamils equal rights or semi-autonomy. Racial equality (hard to come by here) *instead* of secession would probably mean greater economic strength for this small nation. Otherwise, failure to settle racial differences leaves scant alternative to *granting* the *Tamils* autonomy or complete independence.

During previous fighting, then Prime Minister Rajiv Gandhi sent Indian troops to buttress the Sinhalese forces against Tamil separatists. Outside Sri Lanka, a Tamil minority lives in southern India. They exacted revenge against Gandhi by assassinating him in southern India in May 1991 during already violent campaign elections. The repercussions from the fatal action of this tiny minority could be enormous for India. Gandhi's assassination came at a time of profound political uncertainty when the nation was near default on international debts and torn by separatist movements and rising caste and religious tensions.

The potentially catastrophic fallout from a minor and somewhat ignored ethnic conflict in Sri Lanka is a perfect example of the *danger* inherent in *neglecting* ethnic crises anywhere. Recognition and prompt action are required to relieve ethnic tensions before they explode and violence spreads. Often these ethnic hot spots have a long history of neglect and repression leading up to a crisis. Simple ethnic autonomy or independence is the *key* to dissipating generations of hate and violence and establishing a firm base for peace and prosperity.

Assam

Militant secessionists exist in a number of India's 25 states, however those in Assam and Punjab rank among the worst. Because of their instability, both states are ruled directly from India's capital Delhi, with direct help from the army. In the northeastern state of Assam, the driving force for secession is the ULFA (United Liberation Front of Assam), a Marxist outfit operating from the jungles of Myanamar (formerly Burma). ULFA seeks independence for the Assamese people while ignoring the fact a majority of its population may be non-Assamese (No reliable numbers exist to show ethnic distribution here). It's not surprising that one of ULFA's goals is the expulsion of all "foreigners," (non-Assamese), since Assamese might actually be a minority.

Autonomy may be inevitable for Assam, but its economic and political future will be doomed if Marxism is the basis for a new government. Marxism is a further step in the wrong direction from India's already misguided socialist welfare state. Crackdown on the ULFA terrorists is desirable, but it's not easy considering their sanctuary in the jungles and the difficulty in distinguishing look-a-like friends from foes. The future doesn't look bright for Assam. I lived there for a year in World War II, and I grieve for the disintegration that has come to this beautiful region.

Punjab

The Sikh insurgency is the most serious of all secessionist challenges to the central government in Delhi. In large sections of Punjab, militant Sikh secessionists deal in extortion and exercise mafia-like control over the populace. Hindus and Sikhs alike are fleeing as Sikh terrorists were responsible for nearly 3,800 deaths in 1990 and another 1,500 through the first few months of 1991. Many Sikh extremists seek shelter across the border in Pakistan out of reach of the Indian army and police. The leader of the Sikh political party, Simranjit Singh Mann, insists that Punjab must become an autonomous Sikh homeland under the auspices of the UN. However, he also believes an autonomous Punjab loosely federated to India might be acceptable. Punjab is pro-American and offered to send 200,000 Sikhs to fight with coalition partners in the Gulf War.

Autonomy for Punjab seems inevitable and desirable if it can abandon its terrorist tactics in favor of a democratic system. Former Prime Minister Indira Gandhi was assassinated by two of her Sikh bodyguards in 1984 following an Indian Army crackdown at the

Sikh temple in Amritsar. However, turbanned Sikhs are recognized the world over for their industriousness and aggressive free market traits, so there's hope.

Jammu & Kashmir

Potentially the most dangerous of all ethnic conflicts in India is in the state known as Jammu & Kashmir. The Kashmir part of the state is Moslem and adjoins Pakistan in the northwest corner of India. Although politically a part of India, Kashmir's religious and kindred sympathies lie with Pakistan and it's been disputed territory since independence. Pakistan reciprocates with a very paternalistic attitude toward Kashmir which is frequently in direct conflict with Indian policies.

There's been little love lost between India and Pakistan since independence in 1947, and there's a national antagonism borne of centuries of conflict. Pakistan and India have fought three wars since 1947, all of them involving Kashmir. A fourth war could begin at the drop of a hat as tensions are at all-time highs. Again, a seemingly small ethnic problem (like the Tamils in Sri Lanka) could have far-reaching ramifications as India is a nuclear power and Pakistan is close to having the bomb if it doesn't already. A nuclear war in this corner of the world adjacent to China, the USSR and the volatile Mideast could usher in a whole new era of global warfare on a scale threatening man's very survival.

The Kashmir problem should be near the top of the world's agenda. Whether it secedes and becomes an independent nation, merges with Pakistan or simply gains autonomy while remaining federated with India or Pakistan is unimportant in the total scheme of things. What's important is that the conflict gets resolved quickly before another war or possibly a disastrous nuclear exchange occurs. Unfortunately, Kashmir will probably be lost in the maelstrom of India's massive government and economic problems until a crisis occurs. By then it'll be out of control.

Summary

The foregoing are but a few examples of ethnic problems plaguing India. Perhaps India's greatest problem, ethnic conflicts aside, is the legacy of Fabian socialism bequeathed to it by Nehru upon independence in 1947. It has been personified and nurtured down through the years by the Gandhi dynasty from Nehru to his daughter Indira Gandhi and his grandson Rajiv Gandhi. Although the world has tragically witnessed the painful lessons of *centralized* economic systems, breaking the bonds to escape is another matter as the USSR is discovering. Perhaps Rajiv Gandhi's death will serve to break the link in this flawed economic legacy.

Another lesson the world has tragically witnessed is the failure associated with governments based on religious fundamentalism, particularly in Iran. However, a positive aspect of Nehru's philosophy was his belief in a secularist government as opposed to a government based on religious fundamentalism. Major opposition parties to Gandhi's Congress party, the Bharatiya Janata Party and Janata Dal Party, are proponents of socialism and/or religious fundamentalism (Hinduism). Lamentably, India seems to be on a course to repeat both the mistakes of a centralized economy and a government based on religious fundamentalism regardless of who comes to power. India needs a fresh new leader prepared to break with the past and un-afraid to make necessary changes. No one has yet appeared on the horizon. Perhaps Rajiv Gandhi's 20-year-old son, Rahul, or his 21-year-old, Priyanha, will one day return with a reformed legacy and the necessary charisma and mystique to rejuvenate a political dynasty and lead his people on a proper path.

Economic and political instability combined with ethnic conflict means India must seriously consider requests for autonomy or secession by separatists or face the prospect of growing insurgencies and possibly widespread civil war. Referendums take the steam out and can lead to good solutions. Unless India gets its economic and political house in order, its future looks very bleak.

Chapter 15

More Lessons From the Past for Europe's Future

The *European Community*, in its presently evolving structure, cannot and should not be saved. Not even if it were to be integrated into an expanded *European Free Trade Association*. *That's not bad news.* Neither for the entrepreneur, anywhere, nor for the just reborn European democracies—who still find themselves *locked out of the design and construction departments of this New European House.* Having just escaped from one tutelage, these newly sovereign States deserve not to be hoodwinked into serving *new Orwellian masters.*

After 30 years of benign neglect by governments who were only too glad to send their socialists to Brussels, it should surprise no one that the supranational structures they designed "to contain the German clout" are now *irreparably* out of step with the course of history. UK's Margaret Thatcher—and, her successor at 10 Downing Street, plus a growing chorus of European politicians—have not been taken in by *Europhoria.* Instead, they have been looking for ways to keep their organically grown and deeply rooted European countries off the Euro bandwagon.

Forgotten Treaties

A symptomatic and, at that, a particularly unkind cut, is the EC's sly offer to unsuspecting COMECON countries to conclude seemingly advantageous bilateral cooperation agreements. Besides weakening their sovereignty in favor of the EC bureaucracy—for a plate of lentils—many of these agreements would *directly jeopardize the dormant most-favored-nation rights* written into their *old*, still valid, commerce treaties with most EC States.

These treaties constitute real treasures of libertarian principles, providing for tax, commerce, establishment, customs and other *regional freedoms* that some of our peoples can now only dream about. Moreover, they *take precedence over Community law* by virtue of *article 234* of the EC's fundamental *Treaty of Rome*. In fact, the *EC Council, on February 12, 1990, again provided for the official prorogation of 271 commerce treaties* of EC members with other States, some dating back to *1815. These include the invaluable treaties of the United States with all but two EC member States (Portugal and Spain).*

Like Great Britain—with its on-going *"special relationship"* with the US—France, Austria, Switzerland, Malta, Turkey, and the East European countries have *too many valuable cultural and historical assets as well as bridging functions* between Europe and non-European States for them to be *politically plain-levelled.*

They would lose their identity in a crazy quilt design perpetuating discredited socialist policies. The some *200,000 pages of mostly self-serving new regulations the EC produces annually for "guidance" of Europe's entrepreneurs* speaks for itself. Can such a new Tower of Babel *serve* the citizens? The *citizen's* welfare also depends on individuals and enterprises capable and willing to play *viable* markets. Yet, to hassle their players, to regulate markets toward extinction, *continues* to be the bureaucrats' privilege. (His tendency to over-regulate probably springs from a resentment of or jealousy toward the private sector.)

Citizens' Europe

Mobilizing Europe's *dormant potential* requires *de-criminalizing the markets, less bureaucracy, deregulation and even devolution, but not supranationalism, centralization and plain-levelling.* Only the former provide the fertile terrains, the *preconditions,* for needed growth and development in harmony with the environment. With that, open markets, borders, universities and minds and, of course, *real value* currencies, could again work wonders.

What is called for is the Old Continent's responsible *homo oeconomicus*, the *citizen-entrepreneurs*, rather than the aparatchiks here and there, to be again the *masters and driving forces of Europe's future*. Economies, too, can only advance as much and as fast as they succeed in unlocking the *individual's* productivity and creativity—which thrive most in *small* units. For all that to happen, society needs to recognize and honor *again* another human right: the *right to* UNDISCLOSED *private property*.

In contrast, the *present* concepts for encouraging the formerly free citizen to put his capacities to work, and for accommodating the non-EC European countries, testify to *official mediocrity*. They must be *revised* in favor of a *new* EC—the *EUROPEAN CONFED-ERATION*, as proposed by T.G. *Masaryk, Aristide Briand, Gustav Stressmann, Charles de Gaulle, Francois Mitterand, Helmut Kohl* and *Margaret Thatcher*. Indeed, a Magna Carta II is needed. It is to secure the *continent-wide peaceful transition from State tutelage to individual liberties and responsibilities*. Not the bureaucratic, but the historic, cultural and social *"acquis"* of Western and Eastern, Northern and Southern Europe deserve safeguarding.

In the same spirit, e.g., France's, Germany's and Italy's *agricultural* problems might be resolved by honoring their farmers' role as *water guardians*. *Europe's water castle*, Switzerland, could in turn solve its *labor, migrant workers, transit and EC problems* on the basis of its *existing bilateral treaties*. These, incidentally, also provide a *practical alternative* to working out complicated new treaties entailing ratification risks.

Customs-Free Geneva?

E.g., imaginative French Swiss might thus get their hand strengthened vis-a-vis their powerful German counterparts. Switzerland could be asked to *finally honor* old treaty obligations—some providing for the *withdrawal of the Swiss customs from all of Geneva*.

In short, the *boldness* for shaping Europe's future does not require the design of some fancy new framework. Europe may be *redis-*

covered by looking at its roots, by reanimating and applying forgotten old treaties, e.g., on regional *free zones*. It may best be served with a *re-focused, invigorated and enlarged Council of Europe*. And its most effective single manifestation may be found in *placing the public trust back into the individual citizen*, his judgment and, yes, his sense of social responsibility.

In a nutshell: *Give Europe back to its citizens!*

PS: The following is tacked on, not as a real PS but as an appendage to what has gone before.

Yet this wants to be separated, to stand alone, for not only Europeans but people of **every nation** must learn from the mistakes being made in Europe (some with US tax & justice agencies "help"). It is a warning. It is not strictly to do with our book title & basic theme, but if we establish intelligent borders but still have destructive tax laws (time consuming & incentive lacking), we will have defeated ourselves. Our border victories will be of little comfort if we live in a "1984" world with Gestapo tax enforcement of rules that defy all we have learned about economics & psychology.

The footnote below is longer than what it notes, & packs a powerful punch. If you generally ignore footnotes (I often do— shame on me), don't miss this one. In fact, all the footnotes in this volume are more significant than usual. *Smaller nations* tend to have *better* tax rules than big ones—because they are more responsive to their next-door neighbor populations, but until we GET the big nations cut up into small, more responsive size, bear this message in mind.

The following is written by my associate, Anton Keller, who is also Secretary General of the Swiss Investors Protection Association (c.p. 2580, 1211 Geneva 2).

The *LAFFER supply-side curve on tax loans versus tax revenues*, on close analysis and surprisingly, appears to apply as well to such institutions as *democracy*! For the more a society *deprives* its members of their fundamental rights, freedoms and responsibilies—under whatever pretext, such as fighting drugs or tax avoidance[11]—the less they are inclined to develop their inherent potentials.

There are ever more numerous and sophisticated social constraints, laws, regulations and more, purportedly innocent and simple "guidelines" (the stuff the EC bureaucracy produces in avalanches). Actually, the more innocent and sensible they are made to look, the more they are likely to be *wild outgrowths of—always primarily self-serving—bureaucracies*, with ever less constitutional legality and effective legislative control. The clumsy, crushingly voluminous texts bear the formal seal, the imprimatur of constitutional lawmaking, but, make no mistake, little more than that. Present-day *lawmakers here and there have not managed to escape the trappings of the information saturation, thus being dependent on these bureaucracies.*

---

[11] The OECD Convention of December 14, 1960, lists among the aims and purposes of this key organization of industrial countries the "preservation" of individual liberty" (Preamble) and to "maintain and extend the liberalisation of capital movements" (art.2,d). Yet, the *OECD Recommendation on Tax Avoidance and Evasion* of September 21, 1977, calls for strengthening "powers of investigation for the detection and *prevention of tax avoidance"* (emphasis added)—even though the free movement of people and capital to wherever the taxpayer may consider fiscal and other conditions to be more suitable, constitutes an essential human right, a key market factor, and a formal liberty protected by the OECD, Council of Europe, and other statutes fundamental to Western society. In setting up machinery to "combat" sound and entirely legal business practices, as the OECD has done with its Fiscal Committee's most secretive *Working Party No. 8 on Tax Avoidance and Evasion,* the OECD's aims and purposes are seen to be effectively—and increasingly so—*undermined from within, and outside the Member government's and the constitutional lawmakers' real control at that.* This symptomatic phenomenon of our time may have been decisively helped by the manifestly misleading, if not outrightly false French translation in all official OECD documents of the terms *tax avoidance and evasion.* Tax avoidance is legal anywhere and in fact constitutes a key characteristic of the free market; the French translation of these legal key terms into *evasion et fraud fiscal* brought not only confusion for businessmen. With both practices being in most countries subject to criminal proceedings, it opened in fact the *world-wide Orwellian chase of innocent taxpayers* by way of the *supercomputer-assisted international fiscal police,* INTERFIPOL, provided for in the *OECD/Council of Europe Convention on Mutual Administrative Assistance in Tax Matters* of January 15, 1986.

Chapter 16

China

There are more Chinese than any other race or nationality, and they are almost all poor, and of course, vote-less. This massive country begs to be freed & divided. It is and always has been ungovernable through sheer size.

The divisions are fairly easy ones to make. For a start, each province could easily be one country. And in most cases, two to four each.

Take Sichuan, for example. It lies in the heart of China, covers 220,000 square miles, an area slightly larger than France. It has more than 100 million inhabitants, which is double the head count of France and half that of the USA. Sichuan should be at least two countries, if not three or four.

Other provinces, like Guangxi, Yunnan, Hunan, Fujian, Zhejiang, Anhui, Shaanxi, Gansu, Shanxi, Shandong, Jilin, Heilongjiano, Xinjiang, are all very large; all would enjoy the fruits of being separate countries; all could be divided into two, three or four nations.

But it is not just an academic exercise to speak of dividing China at this time, with its totalitarian leadership who won't even allow a peaceful demonstration, much less such radical talk of doing a chop-chop of the chop-suey country? Yes & no. Yes, it's a somewhat shallow gesture for the moment. But no, it's not pointless, because as such thoughts as this begin to circulate through student or academic circles, the ground will be fertilized with these ideas. Just as the Beijing Tiannanmen Square massacre has had a drip-drip effect on both the masses & the leadership, which means it is highly unlikely

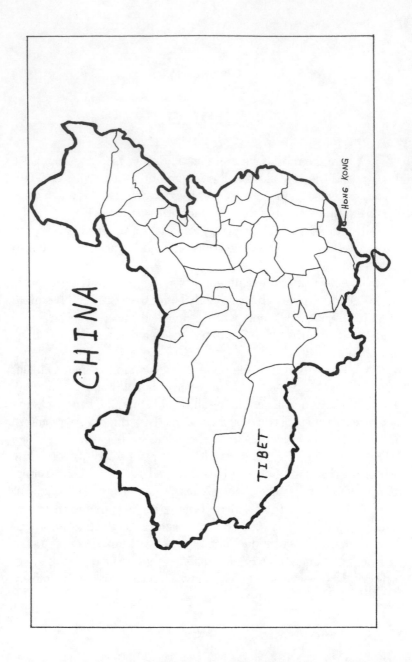

to reoccur. Every action prepares the way for the next action, be it ever so slow.

When the day comes for change in China, these tender ideas may be there waiting. We'll circulate a few copies of this book into Red China to start the intellectual ball rolling. I hope our Hong Kong readers will take a dozen copies with them when they visit China and give them to friends. Let the word begin to spread. Let the journey of a thousand miles begin with one step.

Sadly, we have to include two other countries in this China section even though they are separate countries. But China is pretending they are hers.

Tibet

This lovely, peaceable, inspiring country was ruthlessly overrun & occupied by the communist Chinese army 40 years ago, while the world only tut-tutted over their tea cups. In my view, the world has been far too tolerant of China's abuse of human rights, over and over, simply because it is a BIG country, and they hate to offend big nations. Apparently it is less immoral to offend small ones.

There have been violent uprisings in Tibet in 1987, 1988 and 1989. Or rather they were peaceful demonstrations until the Chinese army made them violent by shooting and beating and jailing demonstrators.

Tibet deserves a place in this book to show solidarity with the Tibetans and to shame the Chinese for occupying the country, and to urge diplomats to step up pressure on China to free Tibet. Statesmen (if there are any left) should include Tibet on their lists of tradeoffs when they dicker with the Chinese over trade. This occupation continues to be a disgrace which all nations share.

Hong Kong

Along with Rhodesia, Hong Kong must go into the record books as the most bungled diplomacy of the century. Hong Kong island is British in perpetuity, i.e., forever. The British wrongly presumed they could not retain Hong Kong island and keep it going as a viable country without the New Territories, which are under lease from Red China. This is untrue, or at least unproven, untested. Many of us contend that China would have continued to supply water and sell vegetables to Hong Kong if they took over the New Territories. To cut off Hong Kong's water would have made Beijing appear a brutal villain (which it is, but likes to pretend it isn't).

Britain should have used this as leverage to get a better deal from China. Either to re-lease the New Territories, or simply keep Hong Kong island and turn over only the N.T. to China under more democratic terms than were obtained. It was horribly botched. It was a giveaway. The UK Foreign Office, once highly skilled, has lost their touch, or else the Prime Minister over-rode the F/O.

In any case, I contend it is NOT too late. The UK can renounce the agreement on grounds of whatever and re-open negotiations. We should be as ruthless diplomatically as the Chinese are in every way. The torment and upset caused by the failure to negotiate something along the lines we have indicated is unforgivable. But amends can be made.

Meantime, all monied Hong Kongese have tried to obtain foreign passports and many have succeeded, and have returned to Hong Kong with their "insurance policy" in their back pocket for use if the Red Chinese prove as nasty in future as they have in the past.

I'm an *"old China hand"* having lived in Shanghai for a year, and visited almost every city in the vast land of China, many years ago. I worked for a local radio station in Shanghai and made enough money playing the Shanghai stock market and the gold markets of China to buy my first newspaper in Palm Springs, California. I received a medal from General Chiang Kai Shek. And I decry the way the US State Dept. sold him out to Mao, ushering in decades of misery for the Chinese people. They are now cowed and brainwashed. The communist dictators murdered millions—not thousands, but millions—of their own people during the uncultural "Cultural Revolution." I hold out little hope for the medium term, since dictators don't give up power just for the asking. I had some hope when

Deng was in charge, but he is too old now, and he has turned his back on his own reforms.

I advocate the West let China go back to sleep, lest the Biblical prophecy come true which says when the sleeping China giant awakes he will make the world tremble. I don't think Nixon should have opened up China although his intentions were good & he was the most skilled foreign affairs president in US history. But it was 200 years too soon. We have lost face by giving in to China, by accepting their dictatorship and rights abuses. They don't respect us because we made *too few* demands. By giving them Most Favored Nation trade status, in return for *nothing*, the US reveals they don't understand the Oriental mentality.

That China should be divided into many *separate nations* is an obvious need, which would *save* the country. But there is no machinery for doing so. They don't have referendums in China. They only have gallows & firing squads. Thus, though we know the *formula* to make the country become happy and prosperous (instead of miserable & poor as it is today), we cannot *apply* the formula. It behooves us to isolate China, the very thing the US State Dept. advises us against. With THEIR record, I'll bet against them 8 times in 10 and be right.

Americans are not good at foreign relations, unlike the British, French, Dutch, Belgians & most Euros. The US is too new a country. Not matured yet. Like 3-year-old whiskey. 80% of US diplomacy has always been wrong headed, although always well intentioned. Americans are the most generous on earth, also friendly, outgoing, helpful, thoughtful. But they are naive, childlike, innocent. It will take another 100 years for the US to mature, in my opinion. Meantime, we should take leaves from the books of older heads.

Getting back to Hong Kong, George Hicks, a HK economist, says HK should fight hard for *autonomy* now, not submit to what has been dished up for them by the London-Beijing accord. That should certainly be done, while we simultaneously try to get London to undertake a basic re-negotiation. Double-ten good luck.

Chapter 17

Some Alarm Signals

*Pacta sunt servanda: "Not invented
here. We have Lex Americana."*

On June 15, 1987, the *U.S. Supreme Court*, ignoring the fervent pleas of the British, French, German and Swiss governments, handed a blank check to the U.S. Administration and the U.S. Judiciary for *disregarding* treaty obligations and channels for obtaining evidence abroad if national means of coercion, such as the subpoena power, promise to be *less "time-consuming and expensive"* (#85.1695). Here, one is tempted to recall a guiding principle an enlightened King wrote way back in 1215:

> *We will not appoint justices,... sheriffs, or bailiffs, except of such
> as know the law of the kingdom and are of a mind to keep it well.*
> (*Magna Carta*, June 15, 1215, art.45).

Indeed, the subsequent stock market crash of October 1987 may be the most costly example to date of events *fueled* by global loss of confidence, *provoked*, perhaps unwittingly, by intolerable *contempt* for universally recognized (and until recently, respected and fundamental), principles of law. The highest U.S. court *undermined*— and continues unabatedly to undermine—the fundamental legal hierarchy, the principle of *pacta sunt servanda*—i.e., treaties must be honored, no matter what.

This opportunistic disregard for fundamental legal principles and treaty obligations formally entered into by the USA also constitutes an illegal arrogation of power. For this blatantly-exercised power not only severely undercuts the U.S. President's treaty-making power, but also flies in the face of U.S. Senate's constitutional advice and consent role and, is *not* seen to be compatible with either the text or the background of the U.S. Constitution's respective provisions.

Indeed, in their *Declaration of Independence* of July 4, 1776, the Representatives of the United States of America invoked notably

"the Laws of Nature," their "unalienable Rights" and "attempts by the [British] legislature to extend an unwarrantable jurisdiction over us"

as "causes which impel them to the separation" and the independent pursuit of "Liberty... Safety and Happiness." Also, the *Constitution of the United States of America* of September 17, 1787, provides[12] a.o.:

The President shall... have power, by and with the advice and consent of the Senate, to make [and abrogate] treaties, provided two-thirds of the Senators present concur (art.2, sec.2, al.2).

The Congress shall have power: ...To define and punish offenses against the *law of nations* (art.1, sec.8, al.10).

No State shall... pass any... law impairing the obligation of contracts [or infringing upon federal or foreign jurisdictions]... No State shall, without the consent of Congress, enter into any agreement [or dispute]... with a foreign power, or engage in war (art.1, sec.10, al.1 and 3).

The judicial power shall extend to all cases, *in law and equity*, arising under this Constitution, the laws of the United States, and treaties made or which shall be made, under their authority (art. 3, sec.2, al.1).

---

[12] Emphasis added; the texts in cornered brackets [ ] constitute interpolations based on the available relevant source material, developed by the author in line with the Salamonic principle.

This Constitution, and the laws of the United States which
shall be made in pursuance thereof; and all treaties made,
or which shall be made, under the authority of the United
States, shall be [in harmony with the law of nations, thus
constituting] the supreme law of the land (art.6, al.2).

The Legal Hierarchy, in Many Places, Evolved Aberrantly

The *U.K. High Court*, on April 4, 1991, upheld an order for Nazir
Chinoy, a manager of the Luxembourg-based BCCI (Bank of Credit
and Commerce Internation) to be extradited to the U.S. to stand
trial for allegedly taking part in a conspiracy to launder profits from
illegal drugs—despite allegations that the evidence against Mr.
Chinoy was obtained in breach of the European Convention on
Human Rights.

Lord Justice Thomas Bingham said, "That convention, for better
or for worse, is not part of the law of this country."[12] The European
Human Rights Convention was ratified by the U.K. Parliament on
March 8, 1951, and while the United Kingdom is indeed bound by
it since it came into force September 3, 1953, legal practice in the
U.K. and in other countries has evolved—some would say
degenerated—to the point of rendering these human rights guarantees void unless they have been explicitly incorporated into the
national law, which is yet to happen.

This is another example[13] of how rules originally intended to
safeguard citizens' interests have been side-swiped, have gradually
been voided, or used only when advantageous to state institutions.
This exclusion rule seems to have its origin in the *1627 Petition of Right*,
whereby the King granted in Parliament that:

---

[13] The Wall Street Journal Europe, April 12, 1991.

[14] One other most notable example being the gradual reversion of the fundamental
principle of exclusive taxation by way of treaties originally intended to prevent
double-taxation but which have become the legal basis for allowing the taxmen
of several countries to hassle the same taxpayer.

No man hereafter be compelled to make or yield any gift, loan, benevolence, tax, or such like charge without common consent by Act of Parliament, and that none be called to make answer or take such oath or to give attendance or be confined or otherwise molested or disquieted concerning the same or for refusal thereof.

Chapter 18

The Last Chapter

*(conclusions, miscellany, potpourri,
forgotten & stop-press items)*

Warning: Any efforts to implement the ideas of this book would be counter-productive if they were introduced as part of some structuring arrangement with UN, IMF or other international or regional body, wherein sovereignty were even partially surrendered.

This book endorses *nationalism, not internationalism*. For as I found in looking up the definition of "internationalism" in an *old* dictionary, one of its common meanings 50 years ago was "the socialist movement." To this end, the left systematically turned the very definition of the two words to their advantage. A "nationalist" became the embodiment of "narrow," "provincial," "brutal," etc., etc., while "internationalists" were "progressive," "visionary" and seekers of "peace."

I also wish to acknowlege that we are aware books were written in 1922 & 1928 putting forth a certain communist strategy for a Soviet Black state & a Soviet Hispanic state in the US. That must be treated with the contempt it deserves, since the Soviets had then & still have their own agenda, which often calls for others to be dupes or fronts for their activities.

Using the natural divisions in society became for the communists what they dubbed "struggle for national liberation." In other words, use "hate" (as Lenin said) to divide people into warring groups based on race, creed, color or even gender. The solution was always

the same: bigger, even more repressive, central governments, ultimately giving way to international or regional bodies, i.e., UN, CSCE,
EC, etc., etc. It is the ancient stratagem of "divide and conquer."

More on Lincoln

Historical note: We made references in chapter one to Abraham
Lincoln, and we questioned his judgment in fighting the US civil
war. Some may think his motives included helping the Blacks (as
well as *forcing* the union to stay together). That conclusion is debat-
able. In 1857, in Springfield, Illinois, Lincoln said, "There is a natural disgust in the minds of nearly all white people to the idea of
an indiscriminate amalgamation of the white & black races. A separation of the races is the only prevention of amalgamation. Such
separation... must be effected by where there is a will there is a way,
& what colonization needs now is a hearty will. Let us be brought
to believe it is morally right to transfer the African to his native clime,
& we shall find a way to do it, however great the task may be."

To the first delegation of black leaders ever to visit the White
House, Lincoln said, in 1862: "You & we are different races. We have
between us a broader difference than exists between almost any two
races...This physical difference is a great disadvantage to us both,
as I think your race suffers very greatly, many of them, by living
among us, while ours suffers from your presence. It is better for us
both, therefore, to be separated." He then urged the black colonization of Central America, i.e., Latin America.

We cite this discomforting material to make clear his motives
in fighting the civil war didn't include helping the blacks but solely
for this notion to "hold the union together," which we claim was
a tragic error of judgment. Now, on to more tranquil subjects.

Size-Wise

How big should a country be? The answer really is: as *small*
as *possible.* What does "as possible" mean? It means it has to be enough
to support itself. In the case of Monte Carlo, which is smaller than

Central Park, New York, the size can be very small because of its fantastic location, mild climate, casino, image, reputation, management, royal family, and tax status. The same size plot in the middle of the Sahara desert would NOT be big enough to be a viable country.

Quebec, on the other hand, is many times larger than is necessary for viability, containing vast resources. Holland is small, flat, without natural resources, but manages well. But if it were only 1/20th the size, it would probably not be viable, unless it became a tax haven.

A country should be as small as possible economically, which will vary from the Amazonian jungles to the snow-covered northern limits of Canada.

The size should also take into account existing races/tribes. If an ancient tribe/race in Africa or Indonesia exists in 300 square miles, then that is probably the proper size for them to have a country. That will pre-presume that such land would have adequate water & agricultural land, for it will have evolved over centuries.

It should probably be big enough to have enough population to fend for itself not only economically but militarily—although this last factor will vary drastically from one region to another depending on its neighbors, on defense treaties with other nations, and on its defensive-friendly topography.

And why "as *small* as" possible? In theory, a country would perhaps be ideal if it were about 10 miles square. For then you could easily keep tabs on your political leaders & could scold them as you passed in the street. You would know if someone needed help for loss of job or an injury or illness, & you could organize local assistance through a church or private donation. The government would not (& should not) get involved in these private matters. Public debt would not get out of control because everyone would know what was going on in the small town capital of say 10 square miles. Most heavily indebted countries are large, where the masses didn't know what was going on with their distant politicians, & tended to think someone else would surely watch them. In a small community you know there *is* no someone else. This also builds a sense of responsibility.

How Many Nations?

Some will say: But by these definitions, we might soon have a thousand countries! So? What is so good about having 184, as we do now? That number is already double the list of a half century ago. Was the old list just right?

I hope we have 1,000 countries within the next 10 years. The urgent need is for at least 500.

I'm having to paint with a wide brush here, because we are seeking to establish a new way of looking at life on this planet. The choices to be made are many & complex, but every choice brings with it a multitude of opportunities, jobs, new responsibilities.

With more people given high level positions, the feelings that go with high office will create a more **responsible society!** You hear the term "he grew into the position." Multiply that by 500 new nations and you will have a more serious-minded, more responsible planet.

I suspect our multiple nations concept will have to **come about** via the grass roots. It is unlikely, based on history, that politicians will initiate such drastic surgery. So it will be up to individuals or groups to start petitions for referendums. To get these issues forcefully before the politicians' eyes, to get these questions on a ballot, this is probably the most logical approach at this stage.

Of course, I hope that the national leaders to whom we have sent this book will see the light and take certain actions along our lines in certain countries where it is already a burning issue.

What we're after is a different mental outlook toward "downsizing" nations in order to create harmony & justice & prosperity.

Norway Join?

In the Europe chapter, I said we'd have more to say on **Norway** here. Norway has withstood the siren calls to join the EC (European Common mkt.). They last voted on it in 1972, and narrowly defeated the idea. It inflamed Norway, caused the prime minister to resign, left scars that have still not healed. Again it is being urged, mainly on fear grounds, that Norway will be left out. That's a silly argument because it can/could join anytime it wished. It is not a now-or-never decision. The nation is still evenly divided on the issue. Trade is not the only question. Norway has only been independent since 1905. Previously it was dominated first by Denmark, later by Sweden. For many Norwegians, *"union"* is a dirty word! Their grandfathers fought to *dissolve* the **union** with Sweden. Norway also has little enthusiasm for the open borders & increased immigration that EC membership would bring. I mention all this here because Norway is showing good sense in being reluctant to join ANY union, since unions are becoming fashionable in certain quarters and people get carried away with the word emotionally, not fully realizing the downside. In the case of the EC, it is transiting from its original Rome Treaty purpose of a common TRADE market into a political-monetary-economic bureaucratic superstate, with a single currency and bank & power in Brussels. The socialists of France are pushing this, and I feel it is counter-productive. If I were advising the Norwegians or the Swiss, I would say: stay out. The EC ain't what it used to be, nor where it was intended, and where it's going you don't want to be. With every union or federalization, comes loss of control, loss of sovereignty, loss of freedom.

Constitution Power

USA: From the pages of the clear-thinking New American magazine comes an ad from Arco Supply Co. of Mokena, Illinois, which pictures George Washington addressing the Constitutional Congress. They quote his words: *"Bind them down with the chains of the Constitution."*

He was right, of course. And they tried. And it worked. For about 125 years. Then came people intent on changing a bit here & a bit there & a bit over yonder. After 215 years there are only a few links of those chains left! Through amendments and interpretations (which then set precedents) and new Congressional laws, and eventually just ignoring the Constitution and operating under Executive Orders, the original Constitution (the finest ever written!) is in shambles. So, by starting *afresh*, with 7-9 new governments, each with its own new Constitution, we can get a fresh set of Constitutional chains for politicians to be bound by. The new constitutions will hopefully last for another 125 years (which takes care of your grandchildren), after which another change will no doubt be needed. This, because we are dealing with human nature, and man's tendency to spoil what he creates, in time.

Hawaii: There is a Hawaiian Independence movement which is now a staple lunch conversation topic there. It's very controversial. The population mix is 24% Caucasian, 24% Japanese, 20% ethnic Hawaiians, 11% Filipino, 5% Chinese. Sooner or later a referendum will be suggested here.

Puerto Rico: The move for PR to become a US state has reached fever pitch. In my view, it would be a large mistake, for both sides. It is a terrible drain on US resources, for no benefit. It is turning the Puerto Rican into a welfare-addicted non-person. It is a free ride for many PRs. It is destroying the character of Puerto Ricans, while costing US taxpayers a lot of money for which there is no gain. Puerto Rico should vote on it, and I hope they will vote for independence. If the US Congress votes on it, I hope they will vote against admission. Of course, the Congress vote is the final word, not the local PR vote, regarding admission.

World Leaders

We are sending copies of this book to a number of world leaders. Ideas have consequences, but as my mother use to say about prayer: "You have to take some human footsteps, too." So we'll put these ideas in the hands of some "shakers & movers." But we can't possibly reach all influential people, in press & politico & schools, so I hope you will spread the word too, via gift copies of this book. Sending copies to media people, legislators, educators, and such will increase the odds of our making the dreams of this book come true, and soon!

Join the Campaign

To encourage such gift giving, here are some giveaway prices, which also illustrates that we didn't write this book to make money, but to circulate the ideas. We have, in fact, given away 75% of the gross book price in commissions to those newsletters who distribute it, leaving us just enough to pay publication, mailing, and research cost, with nothing left for promotion.

If you buy 10 copies of this book, you pay only $15 a copy.

If you buy 50, you pay only $10 a copy. If you buy 100, you pay only $6.00.

If you buy 250: $5.00 a copy. If you buy 500 or more: $4.00.

We'll even mail them for you individually, at no postage cost, if you provide a list of names & addresses.

NOTE: We have set up a foundation to carry forward the ideas in this book, to do additional research on them, to encourage honest debate on them, everywhere. We are not seeking funds. I will fund this work personally for as long as I can & as long as there is sufficient interest. The foundation is: The International Commission for the De-centralization of the World's Nations. US address: P.O. Box 2376, Silver Spring, MD 20915. We will have a presence in Switzerland also, for the moment listed only under my name, at P.O. Box 7337, Zurich 8023.

Other World Areas

As this book is not pretending to be a *complete* survey of the world, there are some places that will have to wait until the first sequel is written. E.g.:

The Philippines: There is a strong case to be made here for chopping up this nation of islands into 3-6 separate nations so that they might be more economically, financially, politically viable. They don't function well now. But the specifics will await a later book.

Along with such places as the *Caribbean islands.* Also the secessionist forces on *Bouganville*, Papua New Guinea. Also East Europe. Also the rest of the Middle East. Also the American and Canadian Indians.

Canadian writer Ian C. Woods wrote: "Probably the most successful nation on the earth is Switzerland, which has no natural resources, just a group of responsible people who have kept their noses out of world affairs since 1515 and who guard their borders, balance their budgets and live within their means. Their products are impeccably produced; their railways run super-efficiently. *Big does not mean great;* small is sometimes a great advantage."

Which reminds us what the vice president of the Scottish National Party (for a **separate Scotland**), Dr. Allan Macartney, said on Dec. 28, 1990: "The record shows that *smaller nations* make the best Europeans."

9 No. American Nations

A book was written in 1981 by Joel Garreau (Avon Books, NY, $9.95) called "The Nine Nations of North America," which is a fascinating title. But the book has no parallels with our book. Even so, it makes some interesting points that, in effect, Canada, Mexico & the US actually function and are divided into rival power blocs, with separate loyalties, interests & plans. His nine segments are Mex-America, The Breadbasket, Ecotopia, New England, The Empty Quarter, Dixie, the Foundry, The Islands, & Quebec.

He makes no suggestions for changes, merely delineates how North America functions. He ignores actual borders, which in the real world we can't do. E.g., he includes *Cuba* in The Islands group along with Miami! Because we live in the real world, I suggest changing the borders, to better match realities. Garreau mentions, for example, that Colorado is two very *different* places, the eastern and western halves. But he doesn't suggest doing anything about it. He merely acknowledges the differences. Despite that, the research in this book could be of value when/if certain groups are planning specific new legal borders & nations.

For some 18 years I have explored the possibilities of *starting* a **new country**, and almost succeeded several times. This book doesn't touch on that subject. But if the new boundaries suggested herein come about, there will be so much NEW freedom generated, it will lessen the urgency of a need for a new Adam Smith type nation. Ironically, the *more* different govts. we create, the less "govt." we will have. Proof of that statement is: If the world were under only ONE govt., there would be no choices, no options, no individual freedom at all! More govts. provide more choices, more options, more differences. As the French say, viva la difference!

Buy Predictions?

If you'd like to keep apace with my geo-political and financial writings on a regular basis (which include stock markets, commodities, bonds and metal markets), I invite you to subscribe to HSL (The International Harry Schultz Letter). Therein I *predict* future events and prices, and I have an 85% batting average for the annual forecasts for the last 25 years. HSL is in its 27th year. Subscription rates are as follows: a lifetime sub., US $2,400; 4-yrs., US $1,000; 2-yrs., US $515; 1-yr., US $275; 6-months, US $159; single copy, US $50. Payable in any currency. Write: HSL, P.O. Box 622, 1001 Lausanne, Switzerland. For sub. information, fax Belgium: (32) 16 535 777.

New Parties Needed

NEW POLITICAL PARTIES will be needed under the new nations plan proposed herein. This may or may not get rid of the machines that currently control national politics in most countries, but it will surely give an opportunity for new parties to form. In the US, for example, most sophisticated people realize the Democrats & Republicans are much the same. Tweedle Dum & Tweedle Dee. Howard Phillips, of Conservative Caucus, has recently formed a new party to get the true conservative voice *heard,* even if not elected. His party would have a far better chance if the US were divided & the current DEM/GOP parties forced to start all over in each area. (For info. on Howard Phillips US Taxpayers Alliance party, write: 450 Maple Avenue East, Vienna, VA 22180, USA.)

I can foresee the possibility of several new parties. There would be *5-9 Presidents* for the various (ex-US) nations & that would almost certainly throw up some quality people who got trampled on in the big *insider* game of present-day US machine politics. Howard Phillips would be one of the new presidents, in my opinion. Most agree the present US presidential job is too much responsibility for ONE man. Under our plan the job would effectively (de facto and de jure) be divided among several top people.

Technical questions on how to *divide up national assets & liabilities* for a separation process are already being hotly debated in Canada & Yugoslavia, among other places. By the time of our sequel book, we'll have access to their thinking. Call it neo-politics. A whole new area of political thought. Sufficient to say that compromises can always be found to highly controversial matters, especially if there is good will on both sides.

Holocaust

If *Israel* had been created *sooner,* perhaps the Holocaust could have been totally or largely avoided. Depriving the Jews of their own country in those pre-Israel years was bad geo-politics.

In this same vein, I hope the *Palestinians* will be given a homeland, in Jordan, which is logical, in my opinion. King Hussein should step down and/or let Jordanians vote on becoming THE Palestinian homeland nation. A vote would almost certainly make that come about. The royal family tradition of Jordan has passed its raison d'etre.

At Any Price?

Be it Iraq today, or Sudan tomorrow, or the US Civil War yesterday, to have people **DIE** so that a country (any country) can stay intact, instead of having two separate (happier) states, is ridiculous. Die for the sake of size? Big is better? Big is beautiful? It's non sequitur. In any case, big is not good at *ANY* price.

It is also akin to saying a divorce should NEVER be allowed.

Change is the only non-variable that is with us from birth to death.

South Vietnam was a fairly happy & certainly healthy country, pre-war, pre-Viet Cong. Forcing it to join North Vietnam, to be a union, did not make it a better nation. Precisely the reverse.

If Only...

Who can say how the USA would have grown/blossomed if Jefferson Davis became president of the Confederation of Southern States, and a peace parley with President Abe Lincoln of the Northern States stopped the fighting; peace declared without mass slaughter having taken place. And then separate growth. I hope someone will be inspired to write a book about what might have been. Would North America have been drawn into fewer wars if there had been two presidents for the two nations, making those decisions? There would not likely have been an invasion of Panama a la 1990, nor probably the conditions that made it seem necessary to George Bush.

We can't know what might have happened "if" the civil war hadn't been fought. But your imagination will tell you there are many possibilities, most of which are extremely pleasant. Different cultures, a la Canada. Different TV, not coast to coast pabulum. Less violence? Less precedent for killing as justified action. Less bitterness. There would be minuses as well as pluses, no doubt, but on balance, I'm certain the pluses would easily win.

What We Need

Europe is better for being 12 nations with unique cultures and customs, not a single country. How boring Europe would be if it were only ONE nationality! The US lost a lot by lowering everyone to a common denominator and trying to wipe out differences of culture between states and races. The rich diversity that existed in the 1880s, even to 1910-20, has been sacrificed to coast-to-coast advertising, TV, media, politics, sameness, mass Americana. Wherever you go in the US, it's just more of the same. We don't need the United States of Europe, but rather the **Europeanization of the USA**. If only Texas had stayed separate and California had never joined the union, and north and south grew alongside each other, instead of being handcuffed together. With the richness and diversity, the several states would today be far more interesting and competitive and service-oriented, and innovative. Nothing significant has been gained by union, not as much as has been lost.

We have a chance to change history now, remedy mistakes of the past, start afresh, solve problems that are otherwise unsolvable (like the out-of-control US debt, Oz debt, Canadian debt, Latin debt, etc.).

Rights of Nations

This next item doesn't especially belong in this book, but on the other hand, it belongs in EVERY book, i.e., it should be repeated by all, on every/any occasion.

Michel Peissel, of Cadaques, Spain, writes, "Unless we challenge the 19th century definitions of what constitutes a nation and its rights over its subjects, the oppression of Kurds, Tibetans, Armenians & countless other minorities will continue.

"The time has come to curtail the right of nations to do as they please with the lives of those minorities who through misfortune, accident, injustice, mistakes or conquest happen to fall within the boundaries of a state.

"If the 'Rights of Man' have been clearly spelled out, it is time for an international conference on the 'Rights [& wrongs] of Nations.' What is needed is a set of rules that can be sanctioned by the right of intervention. These rules must be established by an international body. This and this alone will end the unpardonable suffering and mistreatment of minorities around the world by 'legitimate governments unbridled by any form of international law.'"

He is 100% correct. Although it must not be limited to minorities. There must be *limitations* of what govts. can do *TO* their citizens, minority & majority alike. Let's spread the word on this, too. Legislators please note.

And while you are noting, please observe the equal need for the *right to undeclared assets.* The state must prove the citizen has reported wrongly, not the citizen to declare all. We mentioned this earlier, but not often enough. This right used to be taken for granted. Only in the past 60 years or so has it been slowly reversed. It should be codified in law. Otherwise we have a master/slave relationship between state and citizen. Many have not realized how many freedoms we have lost in this century. I dub the 1900's as the Orwellian Century. How wonderful it would be if we could reverse socialist and Big Brother trends and usher in the 2000's as the *century of the rights of the individual*!

Big & Bad

It is probably no coincidence that the bigger nations are in the vanguard of Big Brotherhood. Orwellianism thrives most in the US, Canada, Australia, England, France, China. Big countries develop big *bureaucracies*, which require big tax receipts to keep them going, which leads to "1984" (i.e., Orwellian) methods of tax assessment and collection. We need more small nations to balance out & ward off Big Brother.

Keep 'em Local!

The lead article in The New American magazine of May 21, 1991 features the story about the Los Angeles black man Rodney King, and his videotaped beating by LA cops. But this story was headlined: *"Keep them local, keep us free,"* which is largely what this book is about. The N/A magazine points out how this LA case has brought up the old cry for a *national* police force with unlimited powers, which they rightly say is "characteristic of totalitarian govts. An oppressive dictatorship can't exist without one, since those in power must have a way to locate and neutralize potential and actual domestic opposition. The Soviet KGB and Nazi gestapo are the best known examples." What they say about police forces is also true of political govt. Keep them LOCAL to keep us free—has been the message of this book from page one. Your chances to control a local govt. or police force are far greater than with a national & distant govt. or national police force answerable to no one locally. (I recommend the New American magazine: P.O. Box 8040, Appleton, Wis. 54913, US.)

Do Away With Passports!

The world got along for thousand of years without passports. People travelled everywhere without a problem. Suddenly in 1912 the Russians introduced them & gradually they spread like the plague. Bureaucrats like them because it gives them a large measure of *control* over the population. Bureaucrats thrive on control.

But the UN implies they aren't necessary! The UN says your right to travel shall not be blocked. The fundamental human right of freedom of movement is defined by United Nations Article 13, in the Universal Declaration of Human Rights.

So passports are not really legal.

Nor are they necessary in any pragmatic sense. Ah, but some say: if we have no passports we'll be flooded with immigrants. That argument is mainly based on race, color or religious prejudice. Or snobbishness. Or ignorance. The facts now available show that immigration (including refugees) does NOT harm the economy of any country where it takes place. Just the reverse.

New research reveals, says Julian Simson, University of Maryland & the Cato Institute, Calif., is author of "The Economic Consequences of Immigration" & founder of the American Immigration Institute. He says: "Immigrants not only *take* jobs; they *make* jobs. Their purchases increase the demand for labor, leading to new hires roughly *equal* in number to the immigrant workers."

See Wall Street Journal Apr. 18, 1991, "Europe's Costly Immigration Myths" by Simon. And Economist magazine of May 11, 1991, on "Yes, they'll fit in too." This is not quite in keeping with the title of this book, but anything that adds substantially to man's freedom merits a place herein. Passports are *not* necessary. They are governmental chains. It is a ghastly joke to believe they serve any purpose that is superior to the harm they do by handcuffing every citizen of every nation.

An incidental benefit would be: enabling people to travel without being singled out by terrorists as Americans (by an anti-US terrorist) or British (by an anti-British terrorist), Israeli (by an Arab terrorist), etc. This would deprive men of violence & give greater/equal safety to all travelers.

It is also an illusion that criminals are frequently apprehended at border crossings. Such occasions are too rare to be worthy of mention.

If the year 2000 is to usher in, as I hinted earlier, a century of individual freedom, we must dispense with passports and ID cards and visas.

Our Aim

This book clearly aims to change the world. That phrase is often used lightheartedly because it seems impossible. But it isn't. Not if right principles & simple truths are employed. We just need to slightly alter the way people look at the nation state, and voila! It's like a large spinning gyroscope can't be moved by using brute force. But if you know where to touch it (gently, with one finger), you can set it spinning in a different direction. The ideas herein offer a challenge to our mental muscle.

I hope you & I have walked a new road herein, leading to or actually being a watershed in geo-political perception. If it is successful, it will reduce violence, increase prosperity, step up representation & unleash new freedoms never before imagined.

Let us try.

Appendix

The following material didn't seem to fit into the foregoing chapters so I include them now as an appendix. They serve as a backdrop against which we carry on our lives. They are not "religious," even though written by two Popes. They have to do with the quality and purpose of life, our priorities and morality. It's slow reading but very much worth the time to do so, unless you want to live the life of a drone, be it a millionaire drone or a peasant drone.

QUOTES from *Centesimus Annus*
The Encyclical Letter by
Pope John Paul II of May 1, 1991

"*Rerum Novarum* (the Encyclica published *100 years ago* by Pope Leo XIII) is *opposed* to State control of the means of production, which reduces every citizen to being a 'cog' in the State machine. It is no less forceful in criticizing a concept of the State which completely *excludes* the economic sector from the State's range of interest and action. There is certainly a legitimate sphere of autonomy in economic life which the State should *not* enter. The State, however, has the task of determining the juridical framework within which economic affairs are conducted, and thus safeguard the prerequisites of a free economy, which presumes a certain equality between the parties, such that one party would not be so powerful as practically to reduce the other to subservience. In this regard, *Rerum Novarum* [and now also: *Centesimus Annus*] points the way to just reform which can restore dignity to work as the free activity of man." (p.31)

Pope Leo XIII, in *Rerum Novarum*, "frequently insists on necessary *limits* to the State's intervention and on its instrumental character, inasmuch as the individual, the family and society are *prior* to the State, and inasmuch as the State exists *in order to protect* their rights and *not stifle them.*" (p.23)

Commenting on the "question of the working class" at a time when "socialism" was "not yet in the form of a strong and powerful State" producing deeply penetrating effects on other societies, institutions and States, Pope Leo XIII recognized "the evil of a solution which, by *appearing* to reverse the positions of the poor and the rich, was in reality *detrimental* to the very people whom it was *meant* to help. The remedy would prove worse than the sickness. *By defining the nature of the socialism of his day as the suppression of private property, Leo XIII arrives at the crux of the problem.*" (p.25/26)

"Widespread drug use is a sign of a serious malfunction in the social system; it also implies a materialistic and, in a certain sense, destructive 'reading' of human needs. In this way the innovative capacity of a free economy is brought to a one-sided and inadequate conclusion. Drugs, as well as pornography and other forms of consumerism which exploit the frailty of the weak, tend to fill the resulting void." (p.72)

"It is not wrong to want to live better; what is wrong is a style of life which is presumed to be better when it is directed toward 'having' rather than 'being', and which wants to have more, not in order to *be* more but in order to spend life in enjoyment as an end in itself. It is therefore necessary to create life-styles in which the quest for truth, beauty, goodness and communion with others for the sake of common growth are the factors which determine consumer choices, savings and investments. In this regard, it is not a matter of the duty of charity alone, that is the duty to give from one's 'abundance', and sometimes give even out of one's needs, in order to provide what is essential for the life of a poor person. I am referring to the fact that even the decision to invest in one place rather than another, in one productive sector rather than another, is always *a moral and cultural choice.* Given the utter necessity of certain economic conditions and of political stability, the decision to invest, that is, to offer people an opportunity to make good use of their own labour, is also determined by an attitude of human sympathy and trust in Providence, which reveal the human quality of the person making such decisions." (p.72/73)

"...the principle of subsidiarity must be respected: a community of a higher order should not interfere in the internal life of a community of a lower order, depriving the latter of its functions, but rather should support it in case of need and help to coordinate its activity with the activities of the rest of society, always with a view to the common good." (p.94)

"By intervening directly and depriving society of its responsibility, the Social Assistance State leads to a loss of human energies and an inordinate increase of public agencies, which are dominated more by bureaucratic ways of thinking than by concern for serving their clients, and which are accompanied by an enormous increase in spending. In fact, it would appear that needs are best understood and satisfied by people who are closest to them and who act as neighbours to those in need." (p.95)

"The individual today is often suffocated between two poles represented by the State and the marketplace. At times it seems as though he exists only as a producer and consumer of goods, or as an object of State administration. People lose sight of the fact that life in society has neither the market nor the State as its final purpose, since life itself has a unique value which the State and the market must serve." (p.97)

The Pope points out "a crisis within democracies themselves, which seem at times to have lost the ability to make decisions aimed at the common good. Certain demands which arise within society are sometimes not examined in accordance with criteria of justice and morality, but rather on the basis of the electoral or financial power of the groups promoting them. With time, such distortions of political conduct create distrust and apathy, with a substantial decline in the political participation and civic spirit of the general population, which feels abused and disillusioned. As a result, there is a growing inability to situate particular interests within the framework of a coherent vision of the common good. The latter is not simply the sum total of particular interests; rather it involves an assessment and integration of those interests on the basis of a balanced hierarchy of values; ultimately, it demands a correct understanding of the dignity and the rights of the person." (p.92)

"A person who produces something other than for his own use generally does so in order that others may use it after they have paid a just price, mutually agreed upon through free bargaining. It is precisely the ability to foresee both the needs of others and the combinations of productive factors most adapted to satisfying those needs that constitutes another important source of wealth in modern society. Besides, many goods cannot be adequately produced through the work of an isolated individual; they require the cooperation of many people in working toward a common goal. Organizing such a productive effort, planning its duration in time, making sure that it corresponds in a positive way to the demands which it must satisfy, and taking the necessary risks—all this too is a source of wealth in today's society. In this way, the *role* of disciplined and creative *human work* and, as an essential part of that work, *initiative and entrepreneurial ability* becomes increasingly evident and decisive." (p.62)

"Indeed, besides the earth, man's principle resource is *man himself*. ... Important virtues are involved in the process to transform man's natural and human environment, such as diligence, industriousness, prudence in undertaking reasonable risks, reliability and fidelity in interpersonal relationships, as well as courage in carrying out decisions which are difficult and painful but necessary, both for the overall working of a business and in meeting possible set-backs.

"The modern *business economy* has positive aspects. Its basis is human freedom exercised in the economic field, just as it is exercised in many other fields. Economic activity... includes the right to freedom, as well as the duty of making responsible use of freedom. ...Whereas at one time the decisive factor of production was *the land*, and later capital—understood as a total complex of the instruments of production—today the decisive factor is increasingly *man himself,* that is, his knowledge, especially his scientific knowledge, his capacity for interrelated and compact organization, as well as his ability to perceive the needs of others and to satisfy them." (p.63)

"Can it perhaps be said that, after the failure of Communism, capitalism is the victorious social system, and that capitalism should be the goal of the countries now making efforts to rebuild their economy and society? Is this the model which ought to be proposed to the countries of the Third World which are searching for the path to true economic and civil progress?

"The answer is obviously complex. If by 'capitalism' is meant an economic system which recognizes the fundamental and positive role of business, the market, private property and the resulting responsibility for the means of production, as well as free human creativity in the economic sector, then the answer is certainly in the affirmative, even though it would perhaps be more appropriate to speak of a 'business economy', 'market economy' or simply 'free economy.' But if by 'capitalism' is meant a system in which freedom in the economic system is not circumscribed within a strong juridical framework which places it at the service of human freedom in its totality, and which sees it as a particular aspect of that freedom, the core of which is ethical and religious, then the reply is certainly negative." (p.81/82)

"Man fulfills himself by using his intelligence and freedom. In so doing he utilizes the things of this world as objects and instruments and makes them his own. The foundation of the right to private initiative and ownership is to be found in this activity. By means of his work man commits himself, not only for his own sake but also *for others* and *with others.* Each person collaborates in the work of others and for their good. ... Just as the person fully realizes himself in the free gift of self, so too ownership morally justifies itself in the creation, at the proper time and in the proper way, of opportunities for work and human growth for all." (p.84/85)

The two coupons below may interest you:

- -

**I would like to link up to HSL (the Int'l Harry Schultz Letter).
Please put me down for:**

- ❑ Life time subscription, $2,400
- ❑ 4 years, $1,000
- ❑ 2 years, $515
- ❑ 1 year, $275
- ❑ 6 months, $159
- ❑ Single Copy, $50

Payment:

❑ Check enclosed

❑ Please charge my credit card:

Company: _____

Card No: _____ Exp. Date: _____

Signature: _____ Date: _____

Name *(as listed on card)* _____

Address *(please print)* _____

_____

_____

- -

International Commission for the De-Centralization of the World's Nations
Washington, DC/Zurich, Switzerland

I want to help the new-borders, freedom, independence causes.

Please note the following suggestions: _____

_____

_____

_____

❑ Tick here if you wish to head up or help a group for some particular
area/cause.

If so, which area: _____

& which cause: _____

Your name *(please print)* _____

Address _____

_____

Phone _____ FAX _____

AIR MAIL

HSL (Harry Schultz Letter).

P.O. Box 622

CH-1001 Lausanne, Switzerland

AIR MAIL

**International Commission for the
De-Centralization of the World's Nations**

P.O. Box 2376

Silver Spring, MD 20915, USA